BOARDS
& SPREADS

SHAREABLE, SIMPLE
ARRANGEMENTS FOR EVERY MEAL

BOARDS & SP

YASMIN FAHR

PHOTOGRAPHS BY JULIA GARTLAND

READS

CLARKSON POTTER/
PUBLISHERS
NEW YORK

To all the home cooks
out there, I hope you
have fun with this book!

CONTENTS

INTRODUCTION

"Let's make a fun spread situation!"

my friend said to me one afternoon, as we chatted about what to eat. We were both feeling a bit lazy in our daytime sweatpants, and didn't want to eat out but also didn't want to cook—quite the modern predicament. A "fun spread" was our answer. A meal for which we could simply buy a bunch of things, doctor them up with a few fresh ingredients and pantry staples to make them feel a bit more homemade, and arrange everything together on a pretty board or platter so that we could nibble, snack, and chat without exerting too much effort or thought for our meal.

I'm a big fan of this style of dining, as I have a "minimal effort, maximum flavor" approach to cooking. I love food that tastes good and making delicious meals, but I don't want to leave the kitchen feeling exhausted afterward, or do a ton of dishes, especially when I have people over.

If that makes you go, "me too!," then welcome to your new favorite book. This low-effort, high-reward cooking approach is also applied to serving those wonderful recipes. Here, you'll find vibrant and flavorful, low-maintenance food spread out on boards or platters for the sake of simplicity and ease. It's a more convenient and casual way to eat, and it looks beautiful, too. While I love a good cheese and charcuterie spread, boards don't need to be relegated to snacks and dips for daytime hangouts or cocktail hour (though you'll find plenty of those here, too), as they work for any meal, any time of day—whether you're gathering around the table for dinner, serving food for a crowd, or planning an outdoor get-together.

You don't need a lot of kitchen skills or experience to make these recipes, as the board-style approach is meant to be low-stress and more about enjoying time with friends and family over a gorgeous (and highly tasty) spread of food than anything else. While everything here is simple to prepare, you'll find that the flavor combinations, colorful food, and serving suggestions make it look and taste anything *but* simple.

This book is built for flexibility, and you are in charge of how small or large the spread becomes—each *key* recipe (i.e., the main thing you're preparing for a given board) can be eaten with as many or as few of the accompaniments, condiments, and suggested sides listed for the board. That way, you won't have to think too much about what goes well with what, as I've done that work for you, and you can scale up or down depending on how many people you're serving.

No matter how you choose to assemble them, you will be able to put these boards and spreads together quickly and easily—preferably while sipping on a drink, so that you can spend more time chatting with friends than working in the kitchen. Soon you'll find that arranging food on big, beautiful boards and platters is one of the most fun (and easy) ways to serve a meal.

Hope you enjoy!

—Yasmin xx

HOW TO USE THIS BOOK

These boards (or platters, or spreads) are designed to let you choose your own adventure in a sense, depending on how many people you are serving or the occasion. You'll find straight-up snacking or appetizer boards, plus add-on options for fuller, more bountiful meals, all with little touches and recipes to lend a more homemade element to your spread. Almost every board in this book consists of one or two "key" recipes—the main component of the board that you will spend a little bit of time cooking—accompanied by a handful of things to serve alongside it. Sometimes those serve-with options are simply garnishes or toppings (lemon wedges for squeezing, an extra bowl of whatever condiment); sometimes they're things you can get at the store, like bread or crackers; and sometimes they're quick recipes that you'll find in the back of the book (Accents + Add-ons, page 150, and Dips, Spreads + More Fun Things,

page 167), like Two-Minute Feta Dip (page 174) or Jammy Eggs (page 161). These add-on recipes act as easy go-tos that you can use to round out the board with various creamy, acidic, or spicy elements. They pair well with countless boards and platters throughout the book, and their flavor profiles are intentionally harmonious so that you can easily mix and match them. If you ever want to create a larger spread from multiple recipes, you'll find some suggestions in Dinnertime Boards (page 98) for pairing various boards and spreads together.

All in all, once you have a handful of ingredients and supplies (more on that later) and learn what to keep on hand (both in terms of ingredients and quick go-to recipes), then you can easily make many of the spreads in this book on repeat.

As a general rule: The best game plan for every board/platter/spread is to make the "for serving" suggestions first, in the order that they are listed, before you make the "key" recipe (unless a recipe says otherwise) as some might need marinating or pickling time. That way, you'll have everything ready at the same time.

WHAT YOU NEED

The whole idea of this book is to make cooking (and serving) easy, so you really don't need a lot of special equipment or tools. The great thing about a board, whether it's one dedicated to serving or your wooden cutting board, is that it can be a perfect vessel for arranging a variety of foods, from toasts to pizza and pancakes for easy serving at the table. Fill the space around the main recipe with small plates and bowls of different shapes and sizes (mismatching gives it character, so go for it!) full of condiments, dips, sauces, and add-ons to create the spread.

You certainly don't need the perfect board, platter, or plate in any case—you only need to be excited about creating a fun spread for people to snack on. I promise you that when you present the food board-style, it will look incredibly appetizing and gorgeous no matter what. Just seeing a spread of colorful food with so many options gets me excited, and I'm sure your friends and loved ones will feel the same.

With that said, it is helpful to have *some* kitchen items for this serving style, and you can pick and choose from the following ideas to find what best suits your style, aesthetic, and, most important, what will actually fit in your kitchen.

BOARDS
Choosing, Caretaking
+ Other Tips

In general, for the recipes in this book, you'll really only need one large board, which can be what you use as your everyday cutting board (especially if you live in a place with little storage space). I recommend using wooden boards for both cutting and serving—they score high in both functionality and visual presentation. For example, I have two Boos Blocks, one light round and one dark rectangular, that I use as my everyday boards and leave out on the counter or propped against the wall for easy access. I also have a beautiful end-grain board from Brooklyn Butcher Blocks that my sister gave me that I love and keep tucked away for more special presentations or occasions. However, some people prefer plastic cutting boards for prep work, so if that's the case with you, then you can use a wooden serving board or platter to serve everything.

If you are someone who has people over a lot, then you might start a collection of marble, slate, or other types of boards, which can be beautiful for serving cheese and charcuterie. While those are gorgeous, you don't necessarily need them for this book, so on page 17 are tips for taking care of everyday wooden boards. And remember, this style of serving food is about making your life easier, so please don't worry or stress about having the right board or serving piece—it will look fabulous covered in delicious food, no matter what.

Board Sizes and Shapes

While one large board will suit your needs for these recipes, if you're interested in a boards "starter kit," I recommend choosing one small square or rectangular wooden (or plastic) board and one larger wooden board of the same shape, or a butcher block (one with a juice groove can be nice, too), in the wood color/variety that you prefer for your kitchen. If you want to add one more, a large round wooden one is both pretty and convenient (that was my most recent purchase). I also have a particular affinity for animal-shaped boards; don't ask me why, but I collect them when I travel (think pig-shaped and fish-shaped ones). These are helpful boards to have when you're arranging smaller portions of food, when you want to bring a board to a picnic, or when you're prepping something small, since these smaller boards are much easier to clean. I love to use animal-shaped boards as my small cutting boards, but a square-shaped one would of course also suffice.

Board Materials

For wooden boards, hard woods, such as maple, walnut, teak, and cherry, are the best choices as they are thick and less water-absorbent, and thicker boards are less prone to warping and cracking. There are a lot of wonderful wooden boards available online, but there are also likely ones in your local stores, where you can find someone to lead you to the best board for your lifestyle and support someone nearby.

Regular Washing

After every use, I first wash the board with a gentle soap, then wipe the board dry with a clean kitchen towel, and finally stand it upright to air-dry completely. Any water or moisture that gets trapped in there can warp the board or make the wood come loose, so you don't want to wash them in the dishwasher or leave them soaking in water. (Cracked boards can also harbor germs and increase the risk of food-borne illness, so it's even better to follow these rules for that reason.)

Long-Term Care

As a general rule, you should ideally do a care day for your wooden board(s) once a month—though that depends on how often you use it, too. It's kind of like giving your board a moisturizing facial, which will keep it looking and operating at its best. On a clean, dry board, use a mineral oil to treat both sides of the board, followed by a food-safe wax—this cleans up knife marks and helps prevent it from warping or the wooden boards loosening. (Most new cutting boards will come with their own recommendation for care.) Admittedly, I cut corners and use a blend of mineral oil, carnauba wax, and natural food-safe beeswax to clean my wooden boards for a two-in-one situation. And to be honest, sometimes I lose track of time and do my board care more like every two to three months—but they are still in great shape, and I've made it thus far in life! However, if you really want to properly take care of your boards and ensure that they will be with you for a long time (a well-cared-for wooden board will ideally last a lifetime), then stick to the monthly care routine or what's recommended for your particular board.

Stains and Smells

Some ingredients, such as turmeric, saffron, and some berries, can leave stains on boards (I can't tell you how many light-colored linen napkins have been lost to turmeric). Consider using only one dedicated side of the board for foods that can stain or arranging those foods on a large plate or on top of bread rather than directly on the board so you don't stain light-colored boards.

If you are serving your meal on the same board as you used for cutting and prepping ingredients, remember that things like garlic, onions, or other alliums will leave an odor behind, which will then unintentionally flavor the other foods you place there—it's especially unpleasant if you slice fruits or desserts on the same part of the board later. No one wants their Citrus-Labneh Pancakes (page 37) tasting like garlic. Dedicate a small board or one side of a board as the onion/garlic/hot pepper section—I marked a little *O* in the corner so that I could remind myself which side was which.

If your board does eventually acquire a stain or odor, then you can do a deep clean by sprinkling the area with salt, halving a lemon and using the cut-side to rub it in until the stain or odor disappears. Rinse it off and dry well.

THE BOARD'S SUPPORTING CAST
Small Bowls, Plates + Other (Mini) Serving Dishes

It's a good idea (and also fun) to stock a variety of sizes when it comes to bowls, plates, or other tiny serving dishes that will hold all the little extras on your board or platter. Here are some ideas for what comes in handy for serving.

Pinch bowls or sugar bowls: Little things like these will always have a place in my heart. Adorable and functional, pinch bowls or sugar bowls are great for much more than sugar—salt, grated cheese, dried oregano, crushed red pepper flakes, or things that easily spill or roll away (like chives or capers). These are the bowls that make it easier to organize and clean up, too.

Shallow four- to six-inch bowls: These are often referred to as cereal bowls or ice cream bowls. They're great for serving crackers or similar nibbles, condiments, and more textured toppings like Quick-Pickled Shallots (page 153) or Lemony Herbs + Onions (page 154). You can also set out these bowls for everyone to create their own portions of things from the board, such as with the Homemade Granola Board (page 41) or the Top-Your-Own Chili Board (page 110).

Shallow eight-inch bowl: This size—in between a so-called cereal bowl and larger family-style serving bowls—is one of my favorites for everyday use. It's size and shape make it perfect for pasta, stews, hummus, saucy side dishes or salads, or putting toasted pitas in.

Little serving or demitasse spoons: I have a large collection of these because I'm obsessed. They are great for serving and also look so cute.

OTHER KITCHEN EQUIPMENT

The list here is short because the recipes in this book really don't require much more than these. Chances are you already have most or all of these standard items anyway, but here are the go-tos you'll want to have:

- **A sturdy half-sheet pan** (18 × 13 inches)
- **A Dutch oven** or other large lidded pot
- **A 12-inch skillet**, preferably cast-iron
- **A Microplane grater** (helpful for grating garlic, ginger, and cheese)
- **Kitchen shears** (helpful for cutting meat as well as herbs)

TIPS FOR PRETTY PLATING + SERVING

Please know that these tips are meant to be helpful and fun, but in no way do I want you to feel pressured to create a "perfect" board—there's no such thing, as this serving style is meant to be casual and simple. You should tailor it to your tastes, style, or whatever serving dishes you have on hand, and ignore anything that feels remotely stressful or doesn't feel true to you. Since the recipes use so many herbs and fresh ingredients, your boards and spreads will be colorful and beautiful no matter what—plus, everything will taste delicious, which is really the most important thing.

Spread out similar colors: For example, don't put green olives next to cornichons or pickled green vegetables. In that same vein, mix up sizes and give height to some things so that not everything is flat. I prefer a more spacious board, rather than one that is super crowded (I find those intimidating to eat), but make whatever you feel happier about.

Split things up: If you have a particularly large table or spread, then you can always split dips, sides, or even bread and crackers between two 4- or 6-inch bowls so that they are at both ends of the spread and the serving flow will be smoother for a bigger group of people (this works for snacking spreads, too).

Make it easy: If you have something that needs to be cut up to eat, say the Crispy Snacky Tortilla Board (page 56), then feel free to slice it on the board before serving. People tend to be intimidated to cut into a perfect thing, so if the host has already taken care of the divvying up, that will encourage everyone else to help themselves.

Size matters: Keep in mind the size of the meal or main ingredient that you're cooking and pick a board that fits accordingly, so that the board won't look too sparse or too crowded.

Finishing touches: It's a good idea to set out olive oil, citrus wedges, and flaky salt for most spreads, so that everyone can finish off their dish as they'd like. Freshly ground black pepper and crushed red pepper flakes never hurt either. Adding fresh herbs also adds a pop of color to the boards. I'm not a fan of adding anything that's inedible, e.g., decorative things like tomatoes on the vine or flowers—always better to save that board real estate for the food. Yes, sometimes garnishes are pretty, but it's better to have ones that you can actually eat. Let's keep it easy and simple, my friends.

INGREDIENT PREP
Quick Tips

You don't need a lot of kitchen experience to make these recipes, but there are a few tips for prepping the everyday, foundational ingredients that you'll see throughout these recipes.

Onions: There are some loose, generally accepted rules for cutting onions, depending on your desired use, but sometimes I break them because I love the textural crunch that onions offer and prefer the look of cutting with the natural lines, which is my go-to onion slice, pretty much no matter the usage. As you'll find on page 22, you can slice onions either with the natural lines of the onion or against them, depending on what you want to do with them.

Cutting with the natural lines: Slicing onions like this tends to make the slices stay firm and intact, so this is a good method if you're roasting the onions or cooking them another way (and you can definitely use this method for pickling, too). Halve the onion through the stem and root end, trim off the ends, peel the onion, then cut along the natural lines of the onion.

Cutting against the natural lines: These slices will fall apart during cooking, so this way of slicing is typically used for salads or any dish in which the onions will be raw (cutting them this way will take away some of their strong oniony taste). Halve the onion through the stem and root end, cut off the ends, peel the onion, then cut against (perpendicular to) the natural lines.

Cutting into rings: Trim the stem end, then peel the skin. Cut in rings, moving toward the root end. (This also applies to shallots.)

Grape or cherry tomatoes: While it's typical to slice through the stem end of the tomato, I like to slice it through its belly/along the equator, which will make for a prettier-looking tomato.

Herbs: Most herbs are delicate by nature, so you want to cut those last, as they bruise easily and darken once they're cut. Since many of these recipes use lots of herbs, you can use clean kitchen shears to cut the herbs quickly to save time on chopping. In most cases, whenever a recipe calls for chopped herbs like parsley, mint, cilantro, or dill, you should be using (chopping) both the leaves and the tender stems. The stems should not go to waste, as they are full of flavor and texture.

SPICES

Salt and Pepper: All salt is kosher unless specified otherwise; sometimes I might have you use a flaky sea salt as a finishing salt, if you have it. Black pepper should always be freshly ground, in a pepper mill.

In addition to salt and pepper, most of the spices in the book you will be able to get at your local grocery store, but if you can't find a certain one, then I recommend the online sources below.

Diaspora Co.: Diaspora Co. is great for many spices and herbs, but in particular they have the best and most fragrant turmeric that I have ever tried. They do add salt to some of their spice blends, so keep an eye out if you're sensitive to salt.

The Spice House: Check them out for a great variety of spice blends, such as za'atar, ras el hanout, and others.

Kalustyan's: This incredible store in NYC has almost any spice that you can think of and is just a pure joy to walk around (they also sell Bulgarian feta in bulk).

BOARDS *for* BREAKFAST

There's something so cozy and inviting about a breakfast spread, especially when you stagger sleepily into the kitchen to be greeted by a full table. But that feeling can be captured anytime of day, so these boards are designed with brunch and breakfast-for-dinner in mind, too. From an uncluttered, everyday granola with fun toppings to a board inspired by bagels and lox brunches to citrusy pancakes with fruity and sweet toppings (one even non–pancake lovers will like, promise), these are spreads that will make you and everyone eating with you excited to get the day started. You might fall in love with individual recipes on the various boards here, too, like the Any-Berry Compote (page 164) or the sheet-pan method for making a large batch of eggs, both of which can easily slip into your weekly routine.

THE JAM PLAN BOARD

SERVES 6

When I used to eat breakfast at the Ottolenghi cafés in London, my favorite thing to order was a toast board that came with a variety of jams and other spreads (their banana jam and homemade version of Nutella were two of my favorites) with toasters set up on the communal tables so you can toast your own bread, which was the inspiration for this board. When setting up this spread at home, I like to serve everything as composed, finished toasts on a board, but you can also place the toppings in small bowls around the board and have everyone top their own toasts.

———— ANY-BERRY TOAST ————
with Ricotta + Black Pepper

Before using, taste the ricotta and season it lightly with salt, if necessary (some ricotta is already salted). You won't need to drain fresh ricotta, but ones that you find in a tub will likely need to be drained so it isn't too watery.

Any-Berry Compote (page 164)

4 slices sourdough or other crusty bread

¼ cup ricotta

Freshly ground black pepper

Make the compote. Toast the bread on both sides until golden brown. Layer each toast with ricotta, followed by the compote, and finish with pepper. Serve the toasts on a board or large platter with any remaining compote on the side.

RECIPE CONTINUES

ANY-BERRY TOAST
with Labneh + Black Pepper

Labneh offers a richly concentrated and creamy base, but ricotta could also be used here.

Any-Berry Compote (page 164)

4 slices sourdough or other crusty bread

¼ cup labneh

Freshly ground black pepper

Freshly grated lemon, orange, or grapefruit zest (optional)

Make the compote. Toast the bread on both sides until golden brown. Layer each toast with the labneh, followed by the compote, and finish with pepper and citrus zest, if using. Serve the toasts on a board or large platter with any remaining compote on the side.

PEANUT BUTTER-TAHINI TOAST
with Caramelized Bananas

In this sort-of-fancy take on a PB and banana sandwich, tahini is swirled into the peanut butter for a double-nutty flavor and topped with jammy, dessert-like bananas. And if you want to use Nutella instead of the peanut butter and tahini mixture, I wouldn't stop you.

Caramelized Bananas (page 163)

4 slices sourdough or other crusty bread

2 tablespoons peanut butter or almond butter

2 tablespoons tahini

Make the caramelized bananas. Toast the bread on both sides until golden brown. In a small bowl, stir together the peanut butter and tahini until smooth. Spread a little bit of the mixture onto each toast and top with the bananas. Serve the toasts on a board or large platter with the remaining spread and bananas on the side.

PEANUT
BUTTER-TAHINI
TOAST

ANY-BERRY
TOAST

THE EGG PITA SANDWICH BOARD

SERVES 6 TO 8

A bacon-egg-and-cheese sandwich is a classic hangover food, something that revives you from misery or gives you that little perk you need to recover. Inspired by the New Yorker in me and my Persian upbringing, this spread is a mash-up of the classic BEC, but served in a pita and without bacon to keep it a bit lighter, plus the condiments and add-ons that you would typically find in a Persian meal—namely herbs and onions. It's ideal for weekend getaways with friends when you need breakfast for a crowd but with minimal effort, as you can set everything out on a sheet pan for everyone to serve themselves (and yes, your sheet pan can absolutely act as the "board" in this case if you want it to).

This method of large-batch cooking for eggs uses one of my favorite tricks—the eggs cook in the residual heat of a hot oven, which cooks them gently and evenly. You can even toast the bread under the broiler (if your broiler is in your oven rather than just below); do that first as it will help your oven reach the right temperature more quickly and use this time to make the serving suggestions.

FOR THE EGGS

1 tablespoon olive oil

6 to 8 large eggs

Salt

½ teaspoon crushed red pepper flakes

½ teaspoon ground cumin or za'atar

FOR SERVING

Lemony Herbs + Onions (page 154)

Scallion Labneh (page 177) or **Herby Yogurt Dip** (page 169)

2 medium heirloom, 2 beefsteak, or 3 campari tomatoes, sliced

2 Persian cucumbers or 1 thin-skinned cucumber, sliced or peeled into ribbons

1 avocado, sliced

2 limes, halved

1 cup crumbled feta, or more as needed

Dijon mustard and/or harissa and/or hot sauce

Simple Green Salad (page 178)

6 to 8 pita halves (or tortillas, slices of bread, or English muffins), lightly toasted

Smoked salmon (optional)

RECIPE CONTINUES

MAKE THE EGGS: Heat the oven to 400°F. Add the olive oil to a sheet pan, tilting it to coat the surface, and place the sheet pan in the oven while it preheats.

Once the oven reaches temperature, crack the eggs onto the sheet pan, keeping them close to the edges as best you can (they will cook faster and better this way). Season lightly with salt, red pepper flakes, and cumin and return to the oven. Add the pita halves to another sheet pan or directly on another rack.

Turn off the heat and let the eggs cook for 5 to 7 minutes, until the egg whites are set and the yolks are still a bit runny. (You can gently shake the pan to see if the whites jiggle or stay firm—if they're not quite firm, cook for 1 to 2 more minutes.)

ARRANGE THE BOARD: Use a firm spatula to cut the eggs into squares, stacking them on the sheet pan or transfering them to small plates or directly to a board. Set out the lemony herbs + onions and scallion labneh in bowls. Place the tomato and cucumber slices on the sheet pan or board and season with salt. Add the avocado slices, season with salt, and squeeze juice of one lime half over the slices. Arrange the feta, condiments, remaining lime halves, and green salad around the sheet pan or board, as desired. Transfer the pitas to the sheet pan or board (you can loosely cover the pitas with a clean kitchen towel to keep warm). Add smoked salmon, if desired. Serve immediately.

THE SHAKSHUKA-ISH SPREAD

SERVES 4

Inspired by shakshuka, a richly spiced North African baked egg dish that has endless variations, this version adds mushrooms and spinach while using some of the ingredients often found in shakshuka, such as harissa and cumin. Eat it on its own or opt for making all the suggested sides for a true breakfast or brunch spread, letting everyone help themselves to the garlicky beans, fresh greens, acidic onions, and crunchy cucumbers to balance out the richness of the feta-dotted tomato sauce. Dunking bread into the warm, saucy eggs is a must, and you can also use the bread to make little sandwiches along with the Herby Yogurt Dip, which cuts some of the sauce's heat, too.

FOR THE BAKED EGGS

2 tablespoons olive oil

1 small red onion, thinly sliced

Kosher salt

¾ pound cremini mushrooms, stemmed and thinly sliced

2 garlic cloves, grated or minced

½ to 1 tablespoon harissa, depending on your heat preference

2 teaspoons ground cumin

1 (24-ounce jar) passata (strained) or 1 (28-ounce) can crushed tomatoes

2 cups baby spinach

6 large eggs

½ cup crumbled feta

¼ cup (packed) fresh parsley, roughly chopped or torn

FOR SERVING

Cucumber, Parsley + Red Onion Salad (page 142)

Garlicky White Bean Salad (page 183)

Herby Yogurt Dip (page 169)

Tortillas or pita bread, lightly toasted (see Tip on page 107)

Za'atar Flatbread (page 172)

Simple Green Salad (page 178)

Harissa

RECIPE CONTINUES

MAKE THE BAKED EGGS: Preheat the oven to 350°F with a rack in the center.

Heat the olive oil in a 12-inch oven-proof skillet over medium-high heat until shimmering. Add the onion and season with salt. Cook until the onion has just started to soften, about 3 minutes. Add the mushrooms, season with salt, and cook, stirring occasionally, until golden brown and the mushrooms have lost some of their moisture, 6 to 8 minutes more. (Lower the heat if the onion threatens to burn at any point.) Add the garlic, harissa, and cumin, stirring until fragrant, about 30 seconds. Add the passata and season with salt, stirring to combine. Adjust the heat to maintain a gentle simmer and continue to cook so that the flavors blend together, about 5 minutes more.

Remove the skillet from the heat. Add the spinach and toss until mostly wilted. Use the bottom of a ladle or spoon to make six small wells in the tomato sauce, then crack the eggs into them. Sprinkle the feta in the spaces around the eggs. Transfer the skillet to the oven and bake until the egg whites are set and the yolks are still a bit runny, 9 to 15 minutes, turning halfway. Check by gently shaking the pan, and, if the egg whites jiggle, then continue to cook for 1 to 2 minutes more until they are firm. Remove from the oven and top with the parsley.

MEANWHILE, ARRANGE THE BOARD: Serve the sides in large bowls, small bowls, or directly on the board, depending on the size. Serve the baked eggs directly in the skillet, placed on the board (or the table) with a trivet underneath.

THE PANCAKES BOARD

Citrus-Labneh Pancakes + Any-Berry Compote + Other Fixings

SERVES 4 TO 6

A twist on lemon-ricotta pancakes, this recipe uses labneh in lieu of ricotta or other dairy, so they get the same fluffy, super moist characteristics of traditional pancakes with a bright, citrusy flavor from lemon and orange juice with a touch of olive oil to smooth it out. Putting out all the possible toppings lets everyone decorate their pancakes as they wish, whether it's with syrup, a pat of butter, or the suggestions below. I love slathering these pancakes with Any-Berry Compote (page 164), but you do you.

FOR THE CITRUS-LABNEH PANCAKES

2 cups all-purpose flour

¼ cup sugar

1 tablespoon baking powder

1 teaspoon baking soda

1 teaspoon kosher salt

2 large eggs

1 tablespoon freshly grated zest + ¾ cup fresh-squeezed juice from 2 to 3 navel oranges

1 tablespoon freshly grated zest + ½ cup fresh-squeezed juice from 3 lemons

1½ cups labneh or full-fat Greek yogurt

¼ cup olive oil, plus more for the skillet

FOR SERVING

Any-Berry Compote (page 164)

Caramelized Bananas (page 163)

Butter, room temperature

Maple syrup, room temperature

Preheat the oven to 200°F.

In a large bowl, whisk together the flour, sugar, baking powder, baking soda, and salt and set aside. In a medium bowl, whisk the eggs, then whisk in the citrus zest and juice, labneh, olive oil, and ¼ cup water until combined. Pour the egg mixture into the flour mixture, then stir just enough so that no visible flour remains. Do not overmix. If the batter looks too thick or thickens as it sits, then stir in a tablespoon at a time of room-temperature water to thin it out.

Heat a large skillet over medium heat until very hot, about 1½ to 2 minutes. Add 1 teaspoon olive oil, swirling the pan to coat. Ladle or pour in the batter, making the pancakes as large as you'd like. Cook until they bubble at the edges and the bottoms are browned, 2 to 3 minutes. Flip and cook until the other sides are lightly browned, about 1 minute more. Transfer the pancakes to a sheet pan and place in the oven to keep warm. (Pancakes will take less time to cook as the pan gets hotter.) Repeat with the remaining pancake batter, using more olive oil for the pan as needed.

Serve the pancakes on a board or large platter, along with the compote, bananas, butter, syrup, or any other additional toppings, as desired.

VARIATION

Boozy Pancakes

If you're a fan of Campari, use ¼ cup Campari in place of the water. The slight bitterness of the aperitif complements the citrus, much like one of my favorite drinks, the Negroni.

THE *SMØRREBRØD*-STYLE LOX BOARD

SERVES 4

This colorful, crowd-pleasing board is inspired by the New Yorker in me who loves smoked salmon and lox and my great memories of eating smoked salmon *smørrebrød*-style, the Danish tradition of open-faced sandwiches, with savory, acidic fixings like pickles and herbs and a crusty bread like sourdough or pumpernickel. This board transports me back to Copenhagen and sitting solo at a café table, sipping on a beer and a shot of aquavit, and snacking on plates of curried herring and cured salmon with a variety of mustards, breads, and butters to choose from.

The best way to serve a similar situation at home is to set out everything on a board—the salmon, the bread, and the fixings—and let everyone make their own *smørrebrød* toasts. Feel free to add microgreens or Lemony Herbs + Onions (page 154) to the mix, too.

Quick-Pickled Shallots (page 153)

Scallion Labneh (page 177)

4 **Jammy Eggs** (page 161)

8 ounces smoked salmon, smoked trout, or gravlax

Whole-grain or Dijon mustard

½ cup fresh dill, for serving

1 tablespoon drained capers

2 tablespoons chopped chives

1 medium cucumber or 1 Persian cucumber, thinly sliced

1 lemon, cut into wedges

Arugula Salad (optional; page 179)

Flaky sea salt

8 slices sourdough, pumpernickel, French country, or rye bread, or bagels, toasted

---

Transfer the pickled shallots directly onto the board and serve the scallion labneh in a bowl on the board. Arrange the jammy eggs on the board or nestle them into empty spaces, if crowded. Place the salmon in the center of the board or in one section (you can divide it into two sections if using a larger board and/or a larger portion of salmon). Arrange the mustard, dill, capers, chives, cucumber, and lemon wedges in small bowls around the salmon or directly on the board. Serve the arugula salad in a medium bowl, if using. Sprinkle the eggs and cucumber with flaky sea salt. Add the bread to the board or serve on the side.

NOTE

If you're serving more than 4 people, then double the salmon amount to 1 pound. Typically, you'll want about 2 ounces of salmon per person.

THE HOMEMADE GRANOLA BOARD

SERVES 4 TO 6

This is a granola that you can eat throughout the week without feeling like you're getting a sugar overload—it's full of simple, good-for-you ingredients (and not too many of them). Granola is always worth making at home, not only because it's a low-key thing to throw together, but also because you can use it as a base for a full breakfast spread and doctor it up with various add-ins, depending on your mood. Mix in any dried fruit after it comes out of the oven: figs, apricots, cherries, or raisins would be great. If you're serving a crowd, put out different dried or fresh fruits in bowls so everyone can customize their own bowl.

FOR THE GRANOLA

2 medium egg whites

¼ cup maple syrup

¼ cup olive oil

½ teaspoon salt

2 cups old-fashioned rolled oats

½ cup raw, unsalted pumpkin seeds

½ cup raw, unsalted almonds, roughly chopped

FOR SERVING

Broiled Fruit (recipe follows)

Caramelized Bananas (page 163)

Yogurt or milk

Honey or honeycomb

Heat the oven to 325°F and set a rack in the center. Line a sheet pan with parchment paper for easier clean up, if desired.

In a large mixing bowl, whisk the egg whites until frothy and bubbly. Whisk in the maple syrup, olive oil, and salt. Add the oats, pumpkin seeds, and almonds and use a wooden spoon or rubber spatula to toss until everything is coated in the syrup mixture.

Spread the granola in an even layer on the sheet pan. Bake until the granola is deep golden brown, stirring every 10 to 15 minutes to ensure even browning, 30 to 40 minutes total. Set aside to cool (it will continue to crisp as it cools).

Transfer the granola to a bowl to serve on a board or large platter. Serve the broiled fruit, caramelized bananas, yogurt, and honey in small bowls around the board, as desired.

RECIPE CONTINUES

NOTE

The granola can be stored in an airtight container for up to two weeks.

BROILED FRUIT

This fruit scores high on the scale of super-simple and surprisingly delicious. I absolutely love grilled fruit, but since not all of us have a grill or can use it year-round, broiling is a great alternative that yields a similar result: the natural sugars of the fruit are drawn out and the texture becomes soft and plush, like the inside of a freshly baked fruit pie. It's ideal for stone fruits that aren't quite ripe or fruits that are a little tart, like pineapple, as broiling it leaves just the sweetness behind. Whatever fruit you choose, resist the urge to season it with anything extra like lemon juice, sugar, or salt until after you've tried it in its pure, plain glory.

TIP For the Homemade Granola Board, make the broiled fruit while the granola cools. I also like to use broiled fruit on oatmeal or as dessert, with some fresh mint and ice cream.

CHOOSE YOUR FRUIT

3 oranges, grapefruit, or other citrus (see Note)

4 to 5 stone fruits (such as peaches, plums, or nectarines), cut into ¾-inch wedges, or 1 pint cherries, pitted and halved (see Note)

1 pineapple, cubed (see Note)

NOTE

Larger wedges of fruit will remain firm, while smaller ones will break down and become jammy.

Heat the broiler to high with a rack 6 inches from the heat source. If using citrus fruits, halve each one and trim the bottom of each half by about ¼ inch so that they can sit flat. Place the fruit on the sheet pan (for stone fruit, the flesh should be facing up). Broil until the fruit is softened and slightly charred, 4 to 5 minutes for stone fruit, 6 to 7 minutes for citrus, or 7 to 8 minutes for pineapple, depending on your broiler strength. Transfer the fruit to the board and let cool slightly before eating. It will keep for up to 3 days in an airtight container.

BLOODY MARY BAR

SERVES 4 TO 6

I love any drink that includes a little bite of food to snack on (hello, martini with olives), and a Bloody Mary is the ultimate way to do that. Beyond olives, I like to fill my Bloody Mary with various combinations of pickled veggies (like dilly green beans or okra, or cornichons), celery, and other crunchy ingredients so that my glass is mostly food—which is the great thing about serving this with a toppings bar so that everyone can fill their glasses as they like (it looks beautiful, too). My version of a Bloody Mary is seasoned with harissa, soy sauce, and fresh cilantro to amp up its savory profile, making it great for both breakfast or an early afternoon beverage. While it's fairly mild, people can increase the heat themselves with more horseradish, jalapeños, or harissa from the board. Vodka is the go-to spirit for these, but you can also use gin or tequila for variations on it.

---

46 ounces tomato juice (about 5 cups)

2 cups vodka (about 475ml)

¼ cup fresh lemon juice

1 tablespoon low-sodium soy sauce

1 tablespoon harissa

¼ cup (packed) fresh cilantro, finely chopped

1 tablespoon drained horseradish

Sea salt and freshly ground black pepper

FOR SERVING

Celery stalks

Cocktail shrimp

Pickled dilly green beans, asparagus, or okra

Cornichons

Olives, such as castelvatrano or stuffed olives

Capers

Sliced jalapeños

Horseradish

Harissa

Lemon and/or lime wedges

Freshly ground black pepper or a pepper grinder

All of the hot sauces in your fridge

MAKE THE BLOODY MARYS: In a large carafe or pitcher, combine the tomato juice, vodka, lemon juice, soy sauce, harissa, cilantro, horseradish, ½ teaspoon salt, and ½ teaspoon pepper, and stir until smooth.

ARRANGE THE BAR: Set out 4 to 6 collins or other tall glasses and a bucket or bowl of ice for serving. Place the garnishes of your choice in small bowls, then arrange the bowls on a large board or platter, letting everyone decorate their glass and season their drink as they wish with more hot sauce, pepper, or horseradish. (You can also leave out a bottle of vodka if people want to top up their glasses with a bit more.)

BREADS
on BOARDS

This chapter is dedicated to bread—and bread-like foods—in all its glorious forms, whether that's spreading things on toast, crisping it in the oven, or using it as a vehicle to scoop up dips and other fun food. While that's the common thread of all the recipes here, they range from snacky appetizer spreads to more substantial boards that are full of vegetables and work for a larger weeknight or weekend meal.

While I often suggest specific types of bread for many of these recipes, feel free to experiment with your favorite varieties. I always love a good French baguette and am very lucky to have some wonderful bakeries near me, but in many cases, a rustic country bread or seedy multigrain breads would work, too. And, in cases like toasts, tartines, and pizzas, while I sometimes like to do more of the topping and assembly before putting out the board—and serve the extra toppings alongside— feel free to let people assemble their own from start to finish, especially if your board has the space for all of the ingredients to be set out.

THE NO-COOK TARTINES BOARD

SERVES 4 TO 6

Tartines—aka open-faced sandwiches—are fabulous bites for snacking on when friends come over (or to make for yourself for breakfast or lunch), and are all about easy assembly and zero actual cooking (which is especially great on hot days!). Here are four of my favorite combinations for tartines—I love the tomato + labneh, radish + feta + mint, and cucumber + cheddar + parsley tartines for refreshing, juicy, crunchy bites; and the prosciutto + ricotta tartine for a creamy, hearty contrast with a sweet note of honey. But these combinations are meant to be fluid and flexible—feel free to get creative by mixing and matching (and see some other suggestions on page 53).

As with the Jam Plan Board (page 27) and the Feta Flatbread Board (page 61), you can either do some pre-assembly of the tartines before serving them on the board, with extra ingredients alongside; or you can set out all the ingredients on the board, with the plain toasted bread, for people to assemble everything as they like.

FOR THE TARTINE BASES

8 slices country-style or crusty bread, such as sourdough

Extra-virgin olive oil, for drizzling

Flaky sea salt

Freshly ground black pepper

Heat the broiler to high. Arrange the bread on a sheet pan and drizzle each slice with olive oil. Toast under the broiler (or in a toaster oven) for 1 to 3 minutes, per side, until golden brown and slightly crisped but still soft. Top the tartines as desired (recipes follow) and finish with a sprinkle of flaky salt and black pepper and additional olive oil, as desired.

RECIPE CONTINUES

TOMATO + LABNEH

¼ cup labneh

1 small heirloom or campari tomato, thinly sliced

¼ teaspoon crushed red pepper flakes or za'atar

¼ cup (packed) fresh basil leaves, roughly chopped or torn, small ones left whole

Divide the labneh between 2 slices of bread. Top with the tomato and sprinkle with red pepper flakes, salt, and black pepper. Top with the basil and drizzle with olive oil. Slice in half, if desired.

RADISH + FETA + MINT

¼ cup crumbled feta

1 or 2 radishes or 1 Persian cucumber, thinly sliced

¼ teaspoon crushed red pepper flakes

¼ cup (packed) fresh mint leaves, roughly chopped or torn

Divide the feta between 2 slices of bread. Top with the radishes, and sprinkle with red pepper flakes, salt, and black pepper. Top with the mint and drizzle with olive oil. Slice in half, if desired.

—— CUCUMBER + CHEDDAR + PARSLEY ——

2 tablespoons mayonnaise

1½ teaspoons Dijon mustard

¼ teaspoon drained horseradish

1 lime, halved

2 ounces sharp cheddar cheese, sliced

1 Persian or other small cucumber, peeled into ribbons or thinly sliced

2 tablespoons fresh parsley, roughly torn or chopped

In a small bowl, combine the mayonnaise, mustard, and horseradish and squeeze the juice of half the lime. (If the lime is large, then squeeze in just a little at a time, taste, and continue.) Stir until smooth and season to taste with salt and pepper. Divide the mustard mixture between 2 slices of bread and spread it in an even layer, then top with cheddar and cucumber. Sprinkle with additional salt and top with the parsley. Slice in half, if desired.

—— PROSCIUTTO + RICOTTA + HONEY ——

4 ounces fresh ricotta (about ½ cup)

2 ounces prosciutto

Honey, for drizzling

Divide the ricotta between 2 slices of bread, spread in an even layer, and season with salt. Top with folded pieces of prosciutto. Season with pepper and drizzle with honey. Slice in half, if desired.

VARIATIONS

Mortadella + crushed pistachio + provolone

Burrata + tomato + basil + za'atar/red pepper flakes

Charred corn + ricotta (or burrata) + basil/mint + red pepper flakes

TOMATO + LABNEH
TARTINE

RADISH + FETA
+ MINT TARTINE

CUCUMBER +
CHEDDAR + PARSLEY
TARTINE

PROSCIUTTO +
RICOTTA + HONEY
TARTINE

THE CRISPY SNACKY
TORTILLA BOARD

SERVES 4 TO 6

These crispy tortillas taste almost like thin-crust pizzas but without the work of rolling them out, so they are perfect appetizers for a crowd as a crunchy snacking board. However, these two versions—the tomato pizza and the broccoli pizza—have also easily turned into dinner when I'm eating by myself, because they're the perfect personal size, too. If you're serving guests, though, you can prep the broccoli and tomatoes ahead of time, assemble the pizzas, then broil them when people arrive. And in addition to the suggested list below, you can serve the pizzas with any other no-cook toppings or anything that you can quickly heat up on the stovetop.

TIP Crisping tortillas in a pan is a trick that my sister taught me, which I am grateful for, as the tortillas get super crunchy and are a perfect finger food. Use this method for quick weeknight dishes with eggs or saucy dishes, or brunch things like the Shakshuka-ish Spread (page 33).

FOR THE CRISPY TORTILLAS

1 pint cherry or grape tomatoes, halved

3 tablespoons olive oil, plus more for the pan and for drizzling

½ teaspoon ground cumin

¾ teaspoon crushed red pepper flakes

Kosher salt

1 large stalk broccoli, trimmed, and florets cut into bite-size pieces (1½ to 2 cups)

Freshly ground black pepper

4 (8-inch) flour tortillas

¼ cup store-bought or homemade pesto

½ cup grated whole-milk, low-moisture mozzarella

½ cup crumbled feta

FOR SERVING

Quick-Pickled Jalapeños (page 153)

Pan-Roasted Mushrooms with Parmesan (page 90)

1 lemon, cut into wedges

Freshly grated Parmesan cheese

Crushed red pepper flakes

½ cup fresh basil, roughly torn or chopped

Extra-virgin olive oil

MAKE THE CRISPY TORTILLAS: Heat the oven to 425°F and line two sheet pans with aluminum foil. Set two racks in the oven, one 6 inches from the broiler and one in the center.

On one sheet pan, toss the tomatoes with 2 tablespoons of the olive oil, the cumin, and ¼ teaspoon of the red pepper flakes and season with salt. On the other sheet pan, toss the broccoli with the remaining 1 tablespoon olive oil and the remaining ½ teaspoon red pepper flakes and season with salt and black pepper. Roast the tomatoes on the top rack and the broccoli on the middle rack, 10 to 15 minutes, until the tomatoes are softened and starting to break down and the broccoli can be easily pierced with a fork.

Meanwhile, dab a paper towel with olive oil and spread on the surface of a 12-inch cast-iron or other large, heavyweight skillet. Place the skillet over medium-high heat, about 1½ minutes, or until very hot. Add a tortilla and cook until the bottom side becomes crisp and brown, about 2 minutes. Use tongs to flip the tortilla and cook the reverse side for 30 seconds more, until lightly browned. Transfer to a cutting board. Repeat with the remaining tortillas (which might cook more quickly than the first), adding more olive oil as needed if it starts to smoke.

Heat the broiler to high. Transfer the tomatoes and their juices to a small serving bowl. Remove the foil, then use a paper towel to wipe up any liquid that might have spread onto the sheet pan. Arrange 2 tortillas on the empty sheet pan and spread with the pesto, top with the broccoli, and sprinkle with the mozzarella. Place the remaining 2 tortillas on the other, now empty sheet pan and sprinkle them with almost all of the feta and some of the tomatoes, sprinkling the rest of the feta on top.

Cook the broccoli pizzas on the rack under the broiler until the cheese melts, rotating halfway through if necessary, 1 to 2 minutes. Remove from the oven and place the other sheet pan with the tomato pizzas under the broiler until the feta is soft and melty, about 2 minutes.

ARRANGE THE BOARD: Meanwhile, arrange the quick-pickled jalapeños, pan-roasted mushrooms, lemon wedges, Parmesan cheese, red pepper flakes, and basil in small bowls around or directly on the board. Set out additional olive oil and serve the remaining tomatoes in a small bowl as well. Transfer all 4 pizzas to a board or large platter. Squeeze a lemon wedge over the broccoli pizzas. Let everyone garnish the pizzas, slice as desired, and serve immediately.

TOMATO CRISPY
SNACKY TORTILLA

BROCCOLI CRISPY
SNACKY TORTILLA

THE FETA FLATBREAD BOARD
with Herbs + Veggies

SERVES 4

Sofreh, a Persian restaurant in Brooklyn, served a lovely homemade flatbread topped with a delicious combo of feta and dressed herbs (which also partly inspired the Lemony Herbs + Onions on page 154). The flavors on that flatbread were so bright, creamy, and delicious that I wanted to re-create it at home to be served in a similar, casual way and turned into a larger spread with the addition of a couple of dishes. Go ahead and make the full recipe of the Lemony Herbs + Onions—you'll only need half of it for this board, but save the other half for another use (like the Avocado Salad on page 181, which goes wonderfully with this dish). While this recipe calls for store-bought naan, you can use your favorite flatbread, focaccia, or even pizza dough to make this. It's one of those things that tastes a lot fancier than it really is—the best, right?

FOR THE FETA FLATBREAD

2 pieces store-bought naan or other flatbread

Herby Yogurt Dip (page 169)

½ cup crumbled feta

½ teaspoon za'atar or sumac

2 scallions, thinly sliced

½ cup **Lemony Herbs + Onions** (page 154)

Flaky sea salt

FOR SERVING

Avocado Salad (page 181)

Jammy Eggs (page 161)

Raw vegetables, such as sliced or quartered radishes, snap peas, or other crunchy vegetables, for dipping

Heat the broiler to high and place a rack 6 inches from the heat source. Lightly toast the naan on a sheet pan under the broiler (or in a toaster oven) until warm and slightly golden, 2 to 3 minutes.

Transfer the bread to a board and spread some of the herby yogurt dip in the center, leaving some space around the edges so it's easy to pick up, and serve any remaining dip in a small bowl on the board. Crumble the feta on top of the bread, sprinkle with the za'atar and scallions and some of the lemony herbs + onions and season lightly with salt. Slice the bread into thin strips (or larger pieces). Serve the remaining lemony herbs + onions, the avocado salad, jammy eggs, and sliced veggies directly on the board or in small bowls around the board, as desired.

TIP While I like to serve the composed bread, if you want to make this more of a free-form setup, you can slice the (plain) bread first and then have people assemble their own flatbreads from start to finish, which is always fun. Arrange the feta, za'atar, scallions, and lemony herbs + onions in small bowls around the board with the bread alongside.

THE TINNED FISH BOARD

SERVES 4 TO 6

Admittedly, I was late to the tinned fish game. It wasn't until I visited Lisbon and walked into a store lined with walls and walls of colorful tinned fish and seafood, or *conservas* as they are called (you've probably seen photos of these beautiful displays), that I was opened up to a whole world of possibilities for preserved seafood beyond the canned tuna of my youth. It is common in many countries around the world to eat tinned seafood—it's inexpensive and makes for a super easy snack or quick meal, especially if you don't have much else in the pantry at a given moment. Tinned fish can be eaten simply out of the can (see the sidebar for tips on that) or dressed up with lots of little bites to eat with it. On a hot day, a cold beer is a great match for this.

Quick-Pickled Shallots (page 153)

4 Jammy Eggs (page 161)

3 tins of your preferred seafood

Extra-virgin olive oil

1 or 2 lemons or limes, cut into wedges

Cornichons or other small pickles

Smashed Olives (page 158), or whole olives

Crusty bread, toasts, and/or saltines or other crackers

Fresh herbs (optional)

Arrange the quick-pickled shallots in small bowls and place on a board or large platter. Place the jammy eggs directly on the board. Open the tinned seafood and place the tins directly on the board (alternatively, drain and transfer the seafood to small bowls, and drizzle with olive oil and lemon juice). Arrange the remaining accompaniments directly on the board or in small bowls around the board, as desired, and serve.

HOW TO SERVE
TINNED SEAFOOD

Tinned seafood can be preserved in a variety of different ingredients, which will affect how you want to serve it—so here are some general tips.

Olive Oil-Packed: For most of this category, such as salmon, tuna, sardines, etc., you can simply open up the tin and let people enjoy it, because the oil will taste good, too. Water-packed tins are also fine, but just know that they won't have quite as much flavor as oil-packed, so you will have to work harder to add flavor (a little bit of acid, Dijon mustard, olive oil, and fresh herbs will do the trick most times—this also works for oil-packed ones, if you want to brighten them up).

Pickled Brines: These are used for tinned mussels, clams, squid, and some other seafood. Drain the liquid, then drizzle with olive oil, lemon juice, and herbs.

Seasoned: Tinned seafood that comes in spiced olive oil, tomato sauce, or other seasonings, is easy to serve right out of the tin, but it never hurts to top with some herbs or feta, if you like.

THE PIZZA TOAST BOARD

Cheesy Toasts + Blistered Tomatoes + Mushrooooms + Jalapeños

SERVES 4

A twist on French bread pizza, this uses blistered tomatoes seasoned with a bit of heat, then topped with cheese, and cooked under the broiler until melted, with the natural acidity of the tomatoes perfectly cutting the richness of the mozzarella. Make it as a large batch for friends when the weather is on the cooler side or a quick dinner for yourself paired with one of the simple salads. The serving suggestions bulk it out, and the mushrooms and jalapeños can be used to top the pizza after it comes out of the oven or simply served alongside. You can make the mushrooms and tomatoes at the same time, or if you'd rather not multitask, you can keep the mushrooms warm in the oven while you finish broiling the pizzas.

FOR THE PIZZA TOASTS

2 tablespoons olive oil, plus more for the bread

¼ teaspoon crushed red pepper flakes

1 pint grape or cherry tomatoes, halved

Kosher salt

4 slices country-style bread or ciabatta

¾ cup grated mozzarella (about 3 to 4 ounces) or more, as desired

¼ cup freshly grated Parmesan

FOR SERVING

Pan-Roasted Mushrooms with Parmesan (page 90)

Quick-Pickled Jalapeños (page 153) or fresh jalapeños, sliced

Arugula Salad (page 179) or Simple Green Salad (page 178)

Freshly grated Parmesan

Crushed red pepper flakes

Extra-virgin olive oil

MAKE THE PIZZA TOASTS: In a medium skillet over medium-high heat, heat the olive oil and red pepper flakes until shimmering. Add the tomatoes, season with salt, and cook, stirring occasionally, until the skins burst and the tomatoes fall apart, about 5 minutes.

Meanwhile, heat the broiler to high with a rack 6 inches from the heat source. Lightly oil the bread and arrange the slices on a sheet pan under the broiler. Gently toast on both sides so that the center is crunchy and no longer soft, about 2 minutes. Remove from the oven and divide the tomatoes among the slices, then top with the mozzarella and Parmesan. Return the sheet pan under the broiler and cook until the cheese melts, about 2 minutes, rotating as necessary.

ARRANGE THE BOARD: Place the mushrooms and jalapeños in small bowls. In a medium bowl, toss the arugula salad with its dressing and place on the board or next to it alongside the mushrooms and jalapeños. Transfer the pizza toasts to the board, along with small bowls of Parmesan, red pepper flakes, and olive oil, as desired.

BE YOUR OWN SAUSAGE HERO SPREAD

SERVES 4 TO 6

Be prepared for your kitchen to smell amazing. The scent of garlic and onion mingling with sausage juices will have your neighbors knocking on your door asking what's for dinner (this actually happened). While I personally call it a sub, you are welcome to say that you're having a sausage hero, roll, hoagie, or whatever you prefer. I know there are a lot of opinions about this, so I'm just going to say do what makes you happy. Whatever the bread of choice is, it's really just a vehicle to enjoy this delicious spread. The broccolini addition makes it a more well-rounded meal, but even a salad does the trick.

1 medium red onion, sliced

8 to 10 garlic cloves, smashed

2 tablespoons olive oil

Kosher salt

1 pound spicy or sweet Italian sausages

FOR SERVING

Cucumber, Parsley + Red Onion Salad (page 142)

Roasted Broccolini with Chiles (page 86)

Arugula Salad (page 179)

¼ cup fresh parsley, roughly chopped

Freshly grated Parmesan or pecorino cheese

Calabrian chili paste or crushed red pepper flakes

4 to 6 hoagies, hero rolls, hotdog or hamburger buns, or other rolls, toasted

Preheat the oven to 400°F.

On a sheet pan, mix the onion and garlic with the olive oil and salt, then add the sausages and toss to coat. Prick the sausages all over with a fork and spread everything in an even layer. Cook until the sausages are well browned and reach an internal temperature of 160°F, 30 to 35 minutes, tossing the onion and garlic halfway through to mix them with the rendered fat.

Transfer the sausage mixture to a board or large platter (or keep everything on the sheet pan to serve). You can either halve the sausages or let everyone slice them themselves. Arrange the sides and accompaniments in bowls and plates around the board, as desired.

TIP You can roast the broccolini in the oven at the same time as the sausages on another sheet pan.

CUCUMBER, PARSLEY, + RED ONION SALAD

ROASTED
BROCCOLINI
WITH CHILES

SNACKING BOARDS + SALAD + VEGGIE PLATTERS

I love vibrant, flavor-packed salads and vegetable-focused dishes, whether as a side dish or for dinner itself. The recipes here range from classic snacking choices for appetizers or cocktail hour, like the Italian Aperitivo Board (page 76) or the Many Mezze Snacking Board (opposite)—although sometimes those can easily become dinner, too—while others are larger seasonal vegetable platters that are highly adaptable. The recipes here aren't complicated or fussy, and the seasonal salads and vegetable platters are meant to be add-ons to other boards—adding a salad or vegetable side is an easy way to turn a board into a full meal or larger spread.

THE MANY MEZZE SNACKING BOARD

SERVES 4 TO 6

Mezze—the style of eating with appetizers and small plates popular in some Mediterranean and Middle Eastern cuisines—are typically served in a communal, snacking kind of format with everything in bite-size form, so they are perfect for this board-style approach. This spread is ideal for having friends over or for a solo dinner. This board is also the perfect match to turn smaller dishes like the Charred Romaine Salad (page 94) into a larger dinner or for adding on to the Kebab Dinner (page 122) for a feast-like spread. As always, the board components here are all suggestions—by no means do you have to make everything listed, because no matter what you will get a variety of flavors and textures. And, if you don't want to cook at all, then you can skip the halloumi in favor of feta, crumbling it in chunks, and drizzling with some olive oil and red pepper flakes.

FOR THE PAN-SEARED HALLOUMI

1 tablespoon olive oil

8 ounces halloumi, cut into 1½-inch cubes

FOR SERVING

Restaurant-Style Hummus (page 170)

Herby Yogurt Dip (page 169)

⅔ cup Castelvetrano olives, whole or **smashed** (page 158)

Quick-Charred Artichokes (page 162)

Za'atar Flatbread (page 172), **Feta Flatbread** (page 61), or toasted pita

1 (7-ounce) can stuffed grape leaves (6 to 8 grape leaves)

2 large heirloom or beefsteak tomatoes, sliced, or 1 pint grape or cherry tomatoes, halved

2 Persian cucumbers or 1 small cucumber, thinly sliced

Flaky sea salt and freshly ground black pepper

Simple Green Salad (page 178)

MAKE THE PAN-SEARED HALLOUMI: In a large skillet over medium heat, heat the olive oil, tilting the pan to coat the surface, until shimmering. Squeeze the halloumi dry with a dish cloth or paper towels, then add to the skillet. Cook the halloumi, undisturbed, until the bottom sides are golden, about 3 minutes. Use a spatula to turn the pieces over and continue to cook until browned on most sides, 1 to 2 minutes more. (It doesn't have to be golden brown all over.) Transfer the halloumi to a board or large platter.

ARRANGE THE BOARD: Serve the dips and olives in small bowls and arrange around the board. (Set out a small bowl for the olive pits, too, if using whole olives.) Arrange the artichokes, bread, and grape leaves on the board, the tomatoes in the center so the juices don't run off, along with the cucumbers, and season with salt and pepper. Serve the salad on the side.

THE ITALIAN APERITIVO BOARD

SERVES 4 TO 6

In the tradition of Italian aperitivo, a food-filled cocktail time that reigns supreme in Milan, bitter or bubbly drinks are served with salty, crunchy food to stimulate the appetite for the meal ahead—which means you're actually being wise and doing your body a favor by setting out this spread of food to enjoy with drinks. (For pre-dinner drinks inspiration, check out the aperitifs on page 131.) The star here is the Crispy Prosciutto Caprese, a twist on the traditional salad, where crunchy prosciutto is a great contrast to creamy mozzarella, ripe tomatoes, and refreshing basil. All of the smaller bites here—olives, pepperoncini, artichokes, cheese, more cured meat—round out the spread, and you can pick and choose your favorites to serve (but bread is a must, either plain or toasted like crostini). I recommend first making the Crispy Prosciutto Caprese, followed by the Marinated Chickpeas (page 182), before assembling the rest of the board, to give those things time to cool and marinate.

FOR THE CRISPY PROSCIUTTO CAPRESE

1 teaspoon plus 2 tablespoons olive oil

6 slices prosciutto (about 2½ to 3 ounces)

1 garlic clove, grated or minced

¼ teaspoon crushed red pepper flakes

½ teaspoon dried oregano

1 teaspoon Dijon mustard

1 tablespoon sherry vinegar or lemon juice

Kosher salt and freshly ground black pepper

2 large tomatoes or 6 campari tomatoes, cut into wedges

1 (8-ounce) ball mozzarella, torn into bite-size pieces

½ cup fresh basil leaves, roughly torn, small ones left whole

FOR SERVING

Two-Minute Feta Dip (page 174)

Marinated Chickpeas (page 182)

Quick-Charred Artichokes (page 162)

½ pound mix of mortadella, prosciutto, salami, or other cured meat, with large pieces folded or cut into bite-size pieces

2 to 4 pepperoncini, drained and thinly sliced

1 small Parmesan wedge, whole or cut into bite-size pieces

½ cup Castelvetrano olives, whole or **smashed** (page 158)

Fresh or dried fruit, such as pears or apples, halved or sliced

6 to 8 ripe figs

1 cup fresh ricotta

Flaky sea salt

Crushed red pepper flakes

Extra-virgin olive oil

Crusty bread, crostini, or crackers

MAKE THE CRISPY PROSCIUTTO CAPRESE: In a large skillet, heat 1 teaspoon of the olive oil over medium-high heat until shimmering. Add the prosciutto in one layer. (It's okay if they overlap slightly as they will shrink down.) Cook, turning the prosciutto once or twice with tongs, until crispy and browned, about 4 minutes total. Transfer to a paper towel–lined plate and let cool.

In a small bowl, whisk together the garlic, red pepper flakes, oregano, mustard, vinegar, and the remaining 2 tablespoons olive oil until smooth. Season to taste with salt and black pepper. Arrange the tomatoes on a board with a juice groove, a large platter, or two medium bowls and tuck the mozzarella into the empty spaces, pulling it into smaller pieces if needed to fit. Drizzle some of the dressing over the tomatoes and mozzarella. Break the prosciutto into bite-size pieces and sprinkle on top along with the basil leaves. Serve the remaining dressing on the side (it's great for dipping bread into).

ARRANGE THE BOARD: Serve the marinated chickpeas in a small bowl and arrange the quick-charred artichokes on the board alongside the caprese. Arrange the cured meats on the board along with the pepperoncini and Parmesan. Place the olives in a small bowl (and set out a small pinch bowl for the pits). Scoop the ricotta in a small bowl and season lightly with salt, a pinch of red pepper flakes, and a drizzle of olive oil. Tuck the fig halves on the board, if using. Arrange the crusty bread around everything and serve.

QUICK-CHARRED
ARTICHOKES

TWO-MINUTE
FETA DIP

MARINATED
CHICKPEAS

VEGETABLE BOARDS + PLATTERS
for Every Season

On weeknights, I love eating mostly vegetables for dinner, combining them with a handful of other ingredients that provide flavor and textural contrast (think crunchiness, creaminess, acidity, etc.) to make them shine. Of course, when you're using peak-season vegetables, they don't need much help to taste good, so these vegetable-focused dishes are super simple for the sake of letting the produce do its thing. Serve the seasonal suggestions together for a colorful and filling spread, and you can round it out by adding some of the suggested small plates from Accents + Add-ons (page 150) or Dips, Spreads + More Fun Things (page 167). For extra protein, you can always serve these dishes with some grilled or roasted meat, seafood, or even halloumi (see page 73) as part of a larger spread with a ton of vegetables, letting everyone serve themselves. Or pick and choose from the seasons to add individual recipes to dinnertime dishes like the Salmon Centerpiece Spread (page 121), Mini Sliders Board (page 102), or the Winner, Winner, Chicken Dinner Board (page 114). I know I keep saying it, but this book is meant to be flexible and fluid, adapting to your needs and appetite, so have some fun mixing and matching them all.

THE SUMMER TRIO PLATTER

FOR SERVING

Baked Pita Chips (page 173),
Za'atar Flatbread (page 172), warm
tortillas, or crusty bread

Scallion Labneh (page 177) or
Herby Yogurt Dip (page 169)

Feta Flatbread (page 61)

Avocado Salad (page 181)

Lemon or lime wedges

Extra-virgin olive oil

Flaky sea salt and freshly ground
black pepper

Crushed red pepper flakes

Crumbled feta

Parmesan, crumbled or cubed

TOMATO SALAD
with Feta + Scallion Dressing

This salad can be made any time of year with juicy cherry or grape
tomatoes, but it reigns supreme during the summer months when
tomatoes are at their peak. Mix and match heirlooms or make it all
Sungolds—much loved for their sweetness and low acidity. Definitely
eat this with some crusty bread or toss in some homemade croutons
(page 95) for soaking up the lingering dressing. A handful of arugula
wouldn't be out of place, either.

SERVES 4

2 scallions, light green and white parts
only, thinly sliced

1 tablespoon sherry vinegar, red wine
vinegar, or lemon juice

¼ teaspoon crushed red pepper flakes

½ teaspoon Dijon mustard

2 tablespoons extra-virgin olive oil

Kosher salt and freshly ground black
pepper

1 pound cherry or grape tomatoes,
halved

½ cup crumbled feta

½ cup (packed) fresh basil, mint, or dill,
roughly torn or chopped

In a medium bowl, whisk the
scallions, vinegar, red pepper
flakes, mustard, and olive oil until
smooth. Season with salt and
black pepper to taste. Mix in the
tomatoes, feta, and herbs and
season as needed and serve.

RECIPE CONTINUES

CHARRED CORN SALAD

with Za'atar Dressing

Charring corn in the skillet caramelizes it, accentuating its natural sweetness, which pairs well with the refreshing bites of cucumber and the earthiness of the za'atar. This accidentally vegan dish would also go nicely with the addition of some crumbled feta, though it can definitely stand alone.

SERVES 4

4 tablespoons olive oil

2 ears of corn, kernels removed

Kosher salt

1 teaspoon za'atar

2 small limes, halved

1 teaspoon Dijon mustard

Freshly ground black pepper

½ small red onion or 1 small shallot, diced (about ¼ cup)

2 Persian or other small cucumbers, diced

½ cup (packed) fresh mint, roughly chopped

In a 12-inch skillet over medium-high heat, heat 2 tablespoons of the olive oil until shimmering. Add the corn and season with salt and ½ teaspoon of the za'atar. Cook the corn, undisturbed, for 2 minutes, then stir and continue to cook for about 8 minutes more, repeating the process of cooking for 2 minutes undisturbed and stirring each time, until the corn starts to brown in spots. Squeeze the juice of half a lime over the corn and season with more salt as needed. Let the corn cool slightly off the heat.

Meanwhile, in a large serving bowl, whisk together the remaining ½ teaspoon za'atar, the juice of 1 lime, the mustard, and remaining 2 tablespoons olive oil until smooth. Season with salt and pepper. Add the onion, cucumber, and corn and toss to coat. Stir in almost all of the mint, reserving some for garnish. Season as needed with salt. Cut the remaining lime half into wedges for serving, and serve the corn in a large bowl or platter.

—— GARLICKY BLISTERED GREEN BEANS ——

Here green beans get coated and cooked in a garlic-and-spice-infused olive oil. You can top it with the Herby Green Sauce (page 157)—or serve it on the side—if you want to fancy it up a bit, but the beans can definitely stand alone, too. If you are using the sauce, then make that first.

SERVES 4

2 tablespoons olive oil

2 garlic cloves, grated

½ teaspoon ground cumin

½ teaspoon crushed red pepper flakes

½ pound green or other similar-shaped beans, trimmed

Kosher salt

Herby Green Sauce (optional; page 157)

In a 12-inch cast-iron or other large skillet over medium-high heat, heat the olive oil with the garlic, cumin, and red pepper flakes until the mixture starts to sizzle and is fragrant. Add the green beans, season with salt, and stir to coat in the olive oil. Cook the beans, undisturbed, for 2 minutes, then stir, turning over the pieces as best you can. Continue to cook for about 7 minutes more, repeating the process of cooking for 2 minutes undisturbed and tossing each time, until the skins blister and the beans are crisp-tender.

Turn off the heat and transfer the beans to a large platter, along with anything at the bottom of the pan. Spoon the herby green sauce over the beans, if using, or serve alongside in a small bowl.

THE FALL/WINTER TRIO PLATTER

FOR SERVING

Za'atar Flatbread (page 172), warm pita, or crusty bread

Restaurant-Style Hummus (page 170) or store-bought hummus

Charred Radicchio Salad (page 95)

Jalapeño Rice (page 108)

Garlicky White Beans (page 183)

Lime or lemon wedges

Crumbled feta

Parmesan, crumbled or cubed

Fresh herbs

Crushed red pepper flakes

ROASTED BROCCOLINI
with Chiles

When I lived in London, I pretty much spent more money than I would have liked at the Ottolenghi cafés when I was too tired to cook. They often had a broccoli with chiles that I loved, and this version is my ode to that dish and all of the other flavorful vegetables that the cafés do so well.

SERVES 4

2 bunches broccolini, ends trimmed, large ones halved lengthwise (or 1 head broccoli, florets cut into bite-size pieces)

1 or 2 fresno chiles or jalapeños, cut into coins (see Note)

2 tablespoons olive oil

Kosher salt and freshly ground black pepper

1 teaspoon ground cumin

1 lemon, halved

Preheat the oven to 400°F.

On a sheet pan, toss the broccolini and the chile with the olive oil, and season with salt, pepper, and the cumin. Roast until the broccolini tips are charred and the stems are easily pierced with a fork, 12 to 15 minutes. Remove from the oven, squeeze half the lemon over the broccolini, and toss to combine. Cut the remaining lemon half into wedges. Transfer the broccolini to a board or large platter and serve with the lemon wedges.

NOTE

If you're sensitive to heat, you can remove the seeds and membranes from the chiles before cooking.

CHARRED CARROTS
with Dill + Labneh

Controversial opinion here, but I don't really like carrots unless they are nice and charred, tender, almost blackened—but rather than roasting them for a long time, you can roast them for just about 20 minutes and then finish them under the broiler. Here, the carrots are tossed with spiced pumpkin seeds for crunch, served on top of tangy, lime-spiked labneh—which becomes warm and creamy under the heat of the carrots—for an immensely satisfying dish. Bread of some sort is an ideal vehicle for scooping up the labneh lingering on the bottom of the plate. Extra herbs and lime wedges on the side are a good idea, too.

SERVES 4

1½ pounds small carrots (about 2 bunches), scrubbed, medium ones halved, large ones quartered lengthwise

3 tablespoons olive oil

Kosher salt and freshly ground black pepper

1½ teaspoons ground cumin or za'atar

½ teaspoon crushed red pepper flakes

½ cup raw, unsalted pumpkin seeds

¾ cup labneh or thick, full-fat yogurt, such as Greek or Skyr

1 lime, halved

¼ cup (packed) fresh dill, finely chopped

Heat the oven to 400°F. Set one rack in the center and another rack 6 inches from the broiler.

On a sheet pan, toss the carrots with the olive oil, then season with salt, black pepper, 1 teaspoon of the cumin, and the red pepper flakes. Roast on the center rack until the carrots are tender and easily pierced with a fork, 18 to 20 minutes.

Heat the broiler to high. Add the pumpkin seeds to the sheet pan with the carrots and broil (on the upper rack) until the carrots are charred in spots and the seeds are toasted, 2 to 3 minutes.

Meanwhile, in a small bowl, combine the labneh with the juice of half the lime, the remaining ½ teaspoon cumin, and almost all of the dill. Spread the labneh in an even layer on a large platter or board and arrange the carrots on top of the labneh and top with the remaining dill. Slice the remaining lime half into wedges to serve alongside.

RECIPE CONTINUES

ROASTED
BROCCOLINI WITH
CHILES

PAN-ROASTED
MUSHROOMS WITH
PARMESAN

CHARRED CAROTTS
WITH DILL + LABNEH

PAN-ROASTED MUSHROOMS
with Parmesan

These mushrooms are highly flavorful and adaptable—swap the Parmesan cheese for pecorino or feta, if you prefer, and top them with almost any herb, like parsley, cilantro, thyme, oregano, or even chives, if you want a bit of color.

SERVES 4

1 pound mushrooms, woody stems removed: cremini and shiitake, thinly sliced, or oyster, maitake, trumpet, or others, cut into ½-inch pieces

Kosher salt

2 tablespoons olive oil

1 tablespoon low-sodium soy sauce

1 lemon, zested and halved

¼ cup grated or shaved Parmesan

Heat a dry, 12-inch cast-iron or other large skillet over medium-high heat until very hot, about 1½ minutes. Add the mushrooms (the pan will look overcrowded and that's fine) and lightly season with salt. Cook, undisturbed, for 2 minutes, then stir and let cook again undisturbed, repeating at 1-minute increments, until the mushrooms are golden brown and have shrunk to lose some of their moisture, about 8 minutes total.

Stir in the olive oil and continue to cook the mushrooms until they're even more browned, about 2 minutes more. Stir in the soy sauce and reduce for about 1 minute, then remove the skillet from the heat and transfer the mushrooms to a board, platter, or a bowl to set on top. Squeeze half the lemon juice over the mushrooms and stir in the zest. Top with the cheese and slice the remaining lemon half into wedges to serve with the dish.

THE SPRING DUO PLATTER

FOR SERVING

Herby Yogurt Dip (page 169)

Two-Minute Feta Dip (page 174)

Jammy Eggs (page 161)
or baked eggs (see page 32)

Crusty bread or crostini

Crumbled feta

Fresh mint, chopped or torn

Flaky sea salt

Crushed red pepper flakes

SNAP PEA SALAD
with Feta + Mint

This is the kind of salad you want to make—with bright, flavorful ingredients and colors—to celebrate the start of spring. The salad combined with the asparagus recipe that follows make for a gorgeous vegetable spread, one that can be bulked up with breads and dips, Pan-Seared Halloumi (page 73), or simply cooked chicken or shrimp. If you want to make this salad ahead, then add the arugula right before serving so it doesn't become too soggy.

SERVES 4

2 teaspoons white miso

2 teaspoons Dijon mustard

¼ teaspoon crushed red pepper flakes

Freshly grated zest and juice of 1 lemon (about 1 tablespoon zest and 3 tablespoons juice)

3 tablespoons extra-virgin olive oil

1 pound snap peas, trimmed and cut on the diagonal

3 cups baby arugula

½ cup crumbled feta, plus more for serving

½ cup fresh mint, roughly chopped or torn, plus more for serving

Freshly ground black pepper

In a large serving bowl, combine the miso, mustard, red pepper flakes, lemon zest, and lemon juice and stir until the miso is incorporated. Whisk in the olive oil until smooth. Add the snap peas and arugula, tossing to coat. Top with the feta and mint leaves and finish with black pepper.

RECIPE CONTINUES

ASPARAGUS

with Blistered Tomatoes + Parmesan

This asparagus loves to be served with a baguette or other crusty bread for scooping up all the saucy flavors, and you can also top it with Jammy Eggs (page 161, cooked for 6½ or 7 minutes) or fried eggs to make it more substantial. The soy sauce provides a subtle splash of umami without overpowering the bright vibrancy of spring asparagus or juicy tomatoes that become sweeter as they blister. Swap the Parmesan for goat cheese, mozzarella, or feta and serve more on the side for everyone to top as they'd like.

SERVES 4

2 tablespoons olive oil

1 small red onion, cut into rings

Kosher salt

1 bunch asparagus, trimmed or snapped (about 1 pound)

1 pint cherry or grape tomatoes, large ones halved

¼ teaspoon crushed red pepper flakes

1 tablespoon low-sodium soy sauce

½ cup grated or shaved Parmesan

In a 12-inch cast-iron or other large skillet over medium-high heat, heat the olive oil until shimmering. Add the onion, season with salt, and cook for 1 minute without stirring. Stir in the asparagus, season with salt, and cook, undisturbed, until the asparagus is slightly blistered on the bottom, 2 to 3 minutes more.

Add the tomatoes, season with salt and red pepper flakes, and cook until the asparagus is crisp-tender and the tomatoes are slightly blistered, stirring halfway, about 4 minutes more. (Lower the heat at any point if the onion is threatening to burn.) Add the soy sauce and cook about 1 minute more, using a wooden spoon to scrape up any bits stuck on the bottom.

Transfer the asparagus mixture to a large platter or board. Top with half the Parmesan, serving the rest in a small bowl on the side.

THE CHARRED SALAD DUO

SERVES 4 TO 6

More salads should be charred, in my opinion, and the hearty leaves of romaine and radicchio stand up well to the heat. Searing the lettuces briefly in a skillet means that the leaves wilt and brown, adding a layer of complexity and crunch. Serve them with the suggestions below or add them to other spreads. A sweet vegetable, like roasted carrots or squash, would be a great addition to the radicchio salad to contrast the bitterness of the leaves.

CHARRED ROMAINE SALAD

FOR SERVING

Pan-Seared Halloumi (page 73)

Jammy Eggs (page 161)

Crumbled feta

Sliced cucumbers

Thinly sliced scallions

Flaky sea salt

Crusty bread

TIP Both salads are best served pre-dressed on a platter, but if you want to serve them on a board, you can place the charred leaves directly on the board with the dressing on the side, along with the other ingredients in small bowls on the board, and let everyone finish their salad as they'd like.

NOTE

You can also make the homemade croutons for this salad, just make them first.

3 tablespoons plus 1 teaspoon olive oil

1 large romaine head or 2 romaine hearts, quartered with cores intact, or 2 little gems, halved

Kosher salt and freshly ground black pepper

1 garlic clove, grated or minced

¼ teaspoon crushed red pepper flakes

¼ teaspoon dried oregano

1 teaspoon Dijon mustard

1 tablespoon sherry vinegar or lemon juice

1 pint cherry or grape tomatoes, halved

½ cup crumbled feta

1 avocado, diced

¼ cup (packed) fresh basil or mint, roughly chopped or torn

In a 12-inch cast-iron or other large skillet over medium heat, heat 1 teaspoon of the olive oil until shimmering. Lightly brush about 1 tablespoon of the olive oil on the cut sides of the lettuce.

Working in batches if needed, place the romaine quarters cut-side down in the skillet and season lightly with salt. Cook until the leaves start to wilt and char, about 2 minutes. Flip and continue to cook on all sides until the romaine is charred all over, 1 to 2 minutes more. Transfer the romaine to a large platter or board.

In a small bowl, whisk together the garlic, red pepper flakes, oregano, mustard, sherry vinegar, and the remaining 2 tablespoons olive oil until smooth. Season to taste with salt and black pepper. Arrange the tomatoes on top of the charred romaine, along with the feta, avocado, herbs, and croutons, if using. Spoon some of the dressing over everything and serve the remaining dressing in a small bowl on the side.

CHARRED RADICCHIO SALAD

Marinated Chickpeas (page 182)

2 cups croutons, store-bought or **homemade**

4 tablespoons olive oil

2 radicchio heads, small ones halved or large ones quartered, cores intact

¼ cup raw, unsalted pumpkin seeds

Kosher salt and freshly ground black pepper

1 teaspoon white miso

1 teaspoon Dijon mustard

Freshly grated zest and juice of 1 lemon (about 1 tablespoon zest and 3 tablespoons juice)

2 cups (packed) baby arugula

Make the marinated chickpeas and croutons. Set aside. In a 12-inch cast-iron or other large skillet over medium heat, heat 2 tablespoons of the olive oil until hot, tilting the pan to coat the surface. Add the radicchio cut-side down and cook, undisturbed, for 3 minutes. Flip and add the pumpkin seeds, season with salt, and cook until the radicchio is charred on all sides, 2 to 3 minutes more. Transfer the radicchio to a cutting board to cool slightly, and let the residual heat of the pan finish toasting the pumpkin seeds while you finish the rest of the salad. Remove the core from the radicchio wedges and cut each wedge into 2-inch-thick strips.

Meanwhile, in a large serving bowl, combine the miso, mustard, lemon juice, and lemon zest with the remaining 2 tablespoons olive oil until smooth. Season with salt and pepper. Add the radicchio, arugula, half of the marinated chickpeas, croutons, and pumpkin seeds to the dressing, tossing to coat well. Season as needed with salt and transfer the salad to the table or a board.

HOMEMADE CROUTONS

1 baguette (fresh or day-old), torn into bite-size pieces

3 tablespoons olive oil, plus more as needed

½ teaspoon crushed red pepper flakes (optional)

½ teaspoon dried oregano (optional)

Kosher salt (optional)

Preheat the oven to 400°F.

On a sheet pan, toss the baguette with 3 tablespoons olive oil until well coated. Use more olive oil as needed. Season with red pepper flakes, oregano, and salt, if using. Spread the baguette pieces in an even layer and bake until crispy and just browned at the edges, 8 to 10 minutes. Remove from the oven and let cool.

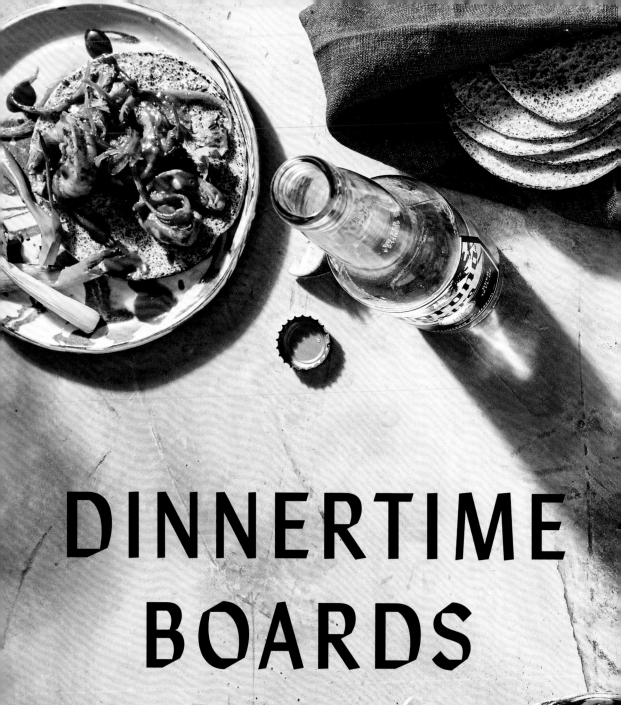

DINNERTIME BOARDS

As embarrassing as this is to admit, in college, someone gave me the nickname "toppings girl." I didn't know him well, but I usually encountered him by the soft-serve ice cream machine at our freshman cafeteria, where a vast toppings bar was set up next to the DIY waffle machine. I loved getting to decorate and dress up my ice cream any way that I wanted, changing it up each time—strawberries swimming in syrup, crunchy bites of chocolate sprinkles, or bits of broken up candy bar and fudge. (And yes, sometimes I even put the ice cream on a waffle.) Each bowl was a chance for something new. Whenever I ran into this guy, he would greet me with "Toppings girl!" I never knew whether to be humiliated by or proud of it.

Anyway, this chapter is meant to channel that toppings-bar energy, as everything here is deconstructed and meant for you to choose-your-own-dinner adventure. You'll find large spreads of food, set up family-style, so that each person can make their own plate or bowl from the myriad of options on the board. Whether you're looking for more substantial meals than the appetizer and veggie boards in the preceding chapters, or you want to make dinner for a crowd but still eat everything board-style for ease of serving (and cleanup), these are the recipes to turn to. As always, please don't feel obligated to make absolutely all of the serving suggestions for toppings and add-ons—you can scale up or scale down the number of dishes depending on how many people you're feeding.

THE MINI SLIDERS BOARD

Chicken Patties with Feta + Herbs

SERVES 4 OR 5

These smashed, feta-filled mini chicken patties are the quintessential board-for-dinner, with mini burger buns and all the much-loved toppings (as well as some twists) set out for people to assemble their own sliders. They're great whether you sandwich the patties with a bun (or other bread) or wrap them in lettuce leaves—after that, throw on some avocado, dollop some Herby Yogurt Dip (page 169) on top, or smear them with harissa (or all of the above). If you have a bit more time (and want to add some crunch from the red onion), instead of plain avocado slices, try the Avocado Salad (page 181) as it makes a great burger or wrap topping, too.

FOR THE CHICKEN PATTIES

Herby Yogurt Dip (page 169)

½ teaspoon harissa

½ cup finely crumbled feta

½ teaspoon crushed red pepper flakes

2 teaspoons Dijon mustard

½ cup (packed) mixed fresh herbs, such as dill, parsley, cilantro, or mint, finely chopped

2 scallions, light green and white parts only, finely chopped

Kosher salt

½ teaspoon ground cumin

Freshly grated zest of 1 lime, with the lime then halved

1 pound ground chicken (preferably dark meat)

3 to 4 tablespoons olive oil, plus more for shaping

FOR SERVING

Mini potato buns/slider buns or pitas, lightly toasted

Butter lettuce leaves or other tender lettuce leaves, such as Boston or Bibb

1 avocado, sliced, or **Avocado Salad** (page 181)

Flaky sea sat (optional)

Lime wedges

Harissa or hot sauce

MAKE THE CHICKEN PATTIES: Combine the herby yogurt dip and the harissa and stir until smooth. Add 2 tablespoons of the harissa-yogurt to a large bowl, and set aside the remaining dip in the fridge until ready to serve. Add the feta, red pepper flakes, mustard, dill, scallions, 1 teaspoon salt, cumin, and lime zest to the large bowl and stir until smooth. Add the chicken and gently mix with your hands until everything is evenly incorporated into the meat. Divide the mixture into 10 portions. Lightly oil your hands and roll the portions into loose balls, slightly larger than golf balls, then use the heel of your palm to smash them into 3-inch-wide patties (about ½-inch thick). Place the patties on a sheet pan or parchment paper.

Heat a 12-inch cast-iron or other large skillet over medium-high heat until very hot, about 1½ minutes. Add 2 tablespoons of the olive oil, swirling the skillet to coat. Add 5 of the patties (do not overcrowd) and cook for 2 to 3 minutes, until browned on the bottom. Use a spatula to flip and cook the patties for 2 minutes more, until well browned on both sides and the inner temperature reaches 165°F. Transfer the patties to a cutting board and squeeze the juice of half the lime over them. Loosely cover with foil to stay warm. Add more olive oil to the skillet as needed and repeat with the remaining 5 patties, squeezing the remaining lime half over them before setting on the board.

ARRANGE THE BOARD: Place the potato buns and lettuce on a board or large platter. Season the avocado slices with salt, if desired, and juice from 1 of the lime wedges and serve them directly on the board or in a small bowl. Serve the reserved harissa-yogurt in a small bowl around the board, along with the lime wedges and any other toppings. Use a spatula to transfer the sliders to the center of the board and serve immediately.

THE TACO BOARD
Chiptole-Spiced Shrimp + Rotisserie Chicken + Tortillas + All the Toppings

SERVES 4 TO 6

This taco spread is great for a crowd, especially if you are serving both meat eaters and pescatarians, as the chicken and shrimp are cooked separately. My all-time favorite shortcut of using a store-bought rotisserie chicken means all you have to do is shred the meat and heat it up with some spices to create a flavorful taco filling. Broiling the shrimp on a sheet pan is perfect for large-batch cooking and only takes a few minutes. You can also choose to make only the chicken or shrimp—the recipes are broken out to make it easy for you. Make as many of the suggested serving items as you'd like, depending on how many you're feeding—and leftovers are delicious eaten as a rice bowl. There is some heat from the chipotle, so this spread is ideal with cold beers served alongside.

FOR THE CHICKEN

2 tablespoons olive oil, plus more as needed

2 garlic cloves, grated or minced

½ teaspoon ground cumin

½ teaspoon dried oregano

1 chipotle in adobo, chopped, plus 1 tablespoon of the liquid

Freshly grated zest and juice of 1 lime

1 (2-pound) rotisserie chicken, shredded

Kosher salt

2 tablespoons fresh cilantro, finely chopped

FOR THE SHRIMP

2 garlic cloves, grated or minced

½ teaspoon ground cumin

½ teaspoon dried oregano

Kosher salt

1 chipotle in adobo, chopped, plus 1 teaspoon of the liquid

Freshly grated zest and juice of 1 lime

2 tablespoons plus 1 teaspoon olive oil

1 pound shrimp, peeled and deveined, tails removed

4 or 5 scallions, trimmed

2 tablespoons fresh cilantro, finely chopped

FOR SERVING

Lemony Herbs + Onions (page 154) (using lime instead of lemon + 1 cup [packed] cilantro)

Quick-Pickled Jalapeños (page 153) or fresh jalapeños, sliced

Jalapeño Rice (recipe follows) or cooked white rice

Charred Corn Salad (page 82)

Hot sauce

Lime wedges

1 avocado, sliced

Corn or flour tortillas, warmed (see Tip)

MAKE THE CHICKEN: In a large skillet over medium heat, heat the olive oil, garlic, cumin, and oregano until the garlic is sizzling, about 1 minute. Stir in the chopped chipotle and the adobo liquid, and the lime zest and cook until fragrant, about 30 seconds. Add the chicken, toss to coat, and cook until warmed through, 2 to 3 minutes more. (Add a bit more olive oil if the skillet looks dry.) Stir in the lime juice, season to taste with salt, and transfer the chicken to a serving bowl to place on a board or large platter (alternatively, transfer the skillet directly to the board) and top with the cilantro.

MAKE THE SHRIMP: On a sheet pan, combine the garlic, cumin, oregano, ½ teaspoon salt, the chipotle and the adobo liquid, the lime zest, half of the lime juice, and 2 tablespoons of the olive oil. Add the shrimp and toss to coat.

Heat the broiler to high with a rack 6 inches from the heat source. On the sheet pan, toss the scallions with 1 teaspoon olive oil and season with salt. Cook until the shrimp are no longer translucent and cooked through, 4 to 5 minutes. (If the shrimp look like they are cooking too quickly, then lower the rack by one level and finish cooking there.) Drizzle the remaining lime juice over the shrimp and top with the cilantro. Transfer the shrimp to a bowl, or serve directly on the board.

ARRANGE THE BOARD: Assemble the accompaniments of your choosing directly on the board or a large platter, or in small bowls. Season the avocado with salt and lime juice, as desired. Serve immediately.

RECIPE CONTINUES

TIP To warm the tortillas, toast them in a dry skillet or use tongs to hold them over an open flame. Wrap the warmed tortillas in foil and keep them warm in the oven while the shrimp cook.

JALAPEÑO RICE

1 tablespoon olive oil

½ teaspoon cumin

1 jalapeño, ½ seeded and diced, ½ thinly sliced

1 cup long-grain white rice, such as basmati or Jasmine, rinsed

Kosher salt

1 cup (packed) fresh cilantro, finely chopped

1 lime, halved

Heat the olive oil and cumin in a medium lidded saucepan over medium-high heat until sizzling, about 1 minute. Add the diced jalapeño, stirring to coat, until just softened and a bright green color, about 1 minute more.

Stir in the rice, coating with the oil, then add 2 cups water and 1 teaspoon salt. Cover, raise the heat to reach a boil, then adjust the heat to low to maintain a gentle simmer, and cook until most of the water has been absorbed, 15 to 18 minutes.

Remove from the heat, and stir in most of the cilantro (leave about 2 tablespoons for garnish), most of the sliced jalapeño, and the juice of half the lime. Season to taste with more lime juice or salt as needed. Top with the remaining cilantro and jalapeño slices.

THE TOP-YOUR-OWN CHILI BOARD

SERVES 4 TO 6

My favorite part about chili is the toppings, which make this untraditional (but delicious) turkey chili so much fun to eat. Flavored with earthy, warming spices from harissa and cumin and with a little extra depth thanks to soy sauce, this one-pot meal can be transferred directly to the table, alongside all of the toppings options. Place these in little bowls or directly on the board for each person to decorate the chili as they wish.

FOR THE CHILI

2 tablespoons olive oil

1 small red onion, diced (about 1 cup)

Kosher salt

2 or 3 large garlic cloves, grated or minced

1 tablespoon ground cumin

1 teaspoon ground turmeric

1 or 2 tablespoons harissa

2 tablespoons tomato paste (preferably double-concentrated)

1 pound ground turkey, or 1 pound turkey sausage (sweet or spicy), casings removed

2 tablespoons low-sodium soy sauce

2 (15-ounce) cans black beans, drained and rinsed

1 small sweet potato, scrubbed and diced

1 quart low-sodium chicken or vegetable broth

FOR SERVING

Lemony Herbs + Onions (page 154) (using 1 cup [packed] cilantro instead of other herbs + ½ teaspoon cumin)

1 cup full-fat yogurt, labneh, or **Herby Yogurt Dip** (page 169)

1 cup grated mozzarella, cheddar, or Monterey Jack cheese

4 scallions, sliced

1 jalapeño, thinly sliced, or **Quick-Pickled Jalapeños** (page 153)

Lime wedges

1 avocado, thinly sliced (optional)

Flaky sea salt

MAKE THE CHILI: In a large Dutch oven or other heavy-bottomed pot, heat the olive oil over medium heat until shimmering. Add the onion, season with salt, and cook, stirring occasionally, until the onion starts to soften in color and texture, about 4 minutes. Stir in the garlic, cumin, and turmeric and cook until fragrant, about 30 seconds. Stir in the harissa and tomato paste and continue to cook to let the flavors mingle, about 1 minute. Add the turkey and stir to coat, using a wooden spoon to break up the meat into smaller pieces. Cook until the meat is well browned and no pink spots remain, about 6 minutes. Stir in the soy sauce and let it evaporate, about 1 minute more.

TIP This chili tastes even better the next day, so make it ahead if you can or freeze it for a future cold day.

Add the beans, sweet potato, and broth. Season with salt and increase the heat to medium-high until the chili reaches a simmer. Reduce the heat to medium-low or low to maintain a gentle simmer, allowing the flavors to blend and the liquid to reduce, about 20 minutes more. (The chili should still be a little brothy.) Season with additional salt to taste.

MEANWHILE, ARRANGE THE BOARD: Place the lemony herbs + onions, the yogurt, cheese, scallions, jalapeño, lime wedges, and avocado, if using, in small bowls or directly on a board or large platter. Season the avocado with salt and lime juice, as desired.

THE WINNER, WINNER, CHICKEN DINNER BOARD

Sheet-Pan Chicken Thighs + Mushrooms + Smashed Garlic

SERVES 4

This sheet-pan dinner offers the benefits of a relaxed serving style plus the ease of oven-to-table cooking. Most of the components here are cooked, rather than raw, as they roast together on the sheet pan—silky onion, golden-brown mushrooms, and smashed garlic cook alongside the chicken thighs and become options for each person to serve the chicken with whatever they want. (And make sure to eat those soft, creamy garlic bits— they are little treasures to be dug up while eating.) You can serve the sheet pan at the table if you want to keep it easy, but if you'd rather transfer this to a board, then slip some toasted pita or naan under the chicken to soak up all the tasty juices.

TIP Smashed garlic (rather than crushed, minced, or grated) gives just enough flavor to a dish without making it overly garlicky. To smash the cloves, place the flat part of your chef's knife over the clove and use the heel of your palm to smash it, much like the Smashed Olives (page 158). Remove the peel and smash one more time if it's not quite there.

FOR THE CHICKEN

2½ pounds bone-in, skin-on chicken thighs

1 lemon

1 medium red onion, thinly sliced

4 to 6 garlic cloves, smashed (see Tip)

3 tablespoons olive oil

Kosher salt and freshly ground black pepper

1 tablespoon za'atar

7 ounces oyster or shiitake mushrooms, ends trimmed and cut into 2-inch pieces

FOR SERVING

Lemony Herbs + Onions (page 154)

Smashed Olives (page 158)

Scallion Labneh (page 177)

Cucumber, Parsley + Onion Salad (page 142)

Arugula Salad (page 179)

Toasted pita, naan, or **Za'atar Flatbread** (page 172)

Lemon wedges

Za'atar (optional)

MAKE THE CHICKEN: Preheat the oven to 425°F and set a rack in the center and one 6 inches from the broiler.

Pat the chicken dry and trim any excess fat. Thinly slice half of the lemon and set aside the other half. On a sheet pan, toss the chicken, sliced lemon, onion, and garlic with 2 tablespoons of the olive oil, seasoning well with salt and pepper. Place the chicken skin-side up and rub all over with the za'atar. Roast on the center rack for 10 minutes.

In a medium bowl, coat the mushrooms with the remaining 1 tablespoon olive oil, seasoning with salt and pepper. Remove the sheet pan from the oven and add the mushrooms, distributing them evenly around the chicken and onion. Return the sheet pan to the oven and cook until the chicken is cooked through (the juices should run clear when pierced with a knife) and the mushrooms are golden brown, 20 to 25 minutes more. If the chicken and mushrooms aren't as crispy as you'd like, then place under the broiler until browned, 1 to 2 minutes more. (You can also add the remaining lemon half cut-side up to the sheet pan to slightly char.)

ARRANGE THE BOARD: Serve the chicken with the lemony herbs + onions, smashed olives, scallion labneh, arugula salad, pita, and lemon wedges, arranging everything around the sheet pan or the board, if using. Sprinkle the scallion labneh with some of the za'atar, if desired.

BIG POT OF MUSSELS ON A BOARD

Curried Mussels + Crusty Bread + Lemony Herbs + Onions

SERVES 4 TO 6

The simplicity and beauty of serving a big pot of steaming mussels to a crowd, having everyone pluck the mussels from the shells, and soaking the bread in the richly flavored broth, is one of the best parts of this communal-style of eating. It's also so easy to make that you can do it for a weeknight dinner, with a salad or veg side you like. The broth is spiced with ginger, scallions, garlic, and curry powder with a creaminess from coconut milk—and is one you might be tempted to drink straight from the bowl, after the mussels are gone. Make sure to set out plenty of dark-colored napkins, because my recommended way to eat mussels is with your hands—use an empty shell to pluck the mussels out of the shells and repeat.

Lemony Herbs + Onions (page 154)

FOR THE MUSSELS

2 tablespoons olive oil

5 scallions (white and light green parts only), chopped

2 or 3 large garlic cloves, grated or minced

1 (1-inch) piece fresh ginger, grated or minced

2 tablespoons curry powder

Kosher salt and freshly ground black pepper

1 (13.5-ounce) can unsweetened full-fat coconut milk

Freshly grated zest and juice of 1 lemon (about 1 tablespoon zest and 3 tablespoons juice)

2 pounds mussels, scrubbed and debearded

FOR SERVING

Crusty bread, baguette, or toasted bread

Lemon or lime wedges

Roasted Broccolini with Chiles (optional; page 86)

Charred Romaine Salad (optional; page 94) or **Charred Radicchio Salad** (optional; page 95)

Charred Corn Salad (optional; page 82)

Make the lemony herbs + onions and set aside.

MAKE THE MUSSELS: In a large lidded pot over medium heat, heat the olive oil until shimmering. Add the scallions, garlic, ginger, and curry powder, season with salt and pepper, and cook until fragrant, about 1 minute. Add the coconut milk, lemon zest, and half of the lemon juice and stir to combine. Add the mussels, cover the pot, and cook until most of the mussels have opened, 5 to 7 minutes. Remove the lid from the pot and add the remaining lemon juice. Stir the mussels

around and discard any that are unopened. Season the broth with salt to taste.

ARRANGE THE BOARD: Place the lemony herbs + onions in a bowl on a board alongside the bread and lemon wedges. Place the pot of mussels on the table or transfer to a large serving bowl, along with small bowls for discarding the shells. Scoop a handful of the lemony herbs + onions and place on top of the mussels, letting everyone add more as they'd like to their individual bowls. Serve immediately.

THE SALMON
CENTERPIECE SPREAD

Simple Roasted Salmon + Herby Green Sauce + Yogurt Dip

SERVES 4 TO 6

A simply prepared salmon is a beautiful centerpiece for a group dinner, especially when it's marinated in Herby Green Sauce (page 157) and served with Herby Yogurt Dip (page 169). While it's quick to put together, you'll have a bit of downtime as the fish bathes in the marinade, which is when you can assemble the suggested accompaniments. I love pairing this with Roasted Broccolini with Chiles (page 86), which you can put in the oven at the same time with the salmon on another rack, or one of the Two Super Simple Salads (page 178). If you have leftover salmon, then it works wonderfully on top of rice or a salad the next day.

FOR THE SIMPLE ROASTED SALMON

Herby Green Sauce (page 157)

1 (2-pound) fillet of salmon, kept whole, skin on or off

1 tablespoon olive oil

Kosher salt and freshly ground black pepper

FOR SERVING

Herby Yogurt Dip (page 169)

Crusty bread or Jalapeño Rice (page 108)

Roasted Broccolini with Chiles (page 86)

Lemon wedges

MAKE THE SIMPLE ROASTED SALMON: Make the herby green sauce. Pat the salmon dry with paper towels. Rub the olive oil onto a sheet pan to coat. Season the salmon all over with salt and pepper. Place the salmon skin-side down on the sheet pan, then cover the flesh with half of the herby green sauce. Let marinate at room temperature for at least 30 minutes or in the refrigerator for up to 2 hours before cooking. Cover the remaining herby green sauce and store in the refrigerator until ready to serve.

Preheat the oven to 400°F and place a rack in the center.

Cook the salmon for 15 to 20 minutes, depending on the thickness (15 minutes will be closer to medium-rare and 20 minutes will be more medium), or until the thickest part of the salmon reaches 120°F for medium-rare. Serve the salmon on the sheet pan, or transfer to a large platter. Let rest for 5 minutes before serving.

ARRANGE THE BOARD: Serve the remaining herby green sauce in a small bowl alongside the salmon, and spoon some on top. Serve the remaining accompaniments on a board or in small bowls around the salmon, as desired.

THE KEBAB DINNER

Turmeric Chicken + Spicy Shrimp + Halloumi + Pitas

SERVES 4 TO 6

While these aren't technically kebabs, as they aren't skewered, the serve-yourself-style with a spread of different ingredients is wonderful for a casual meal, whether indoors or outside. Here, everything cooks together on a sheet pan with the toppings, salads, and add-ons set up around it. Whether you're cooking for omnivores, pescatarians, or vegetarians, there are three options for any type of eater—chicken, shrimp, and halloumi—so make all three for variety's sake or pick and choose as you need to. It might feel like a lot to do, so I suggest starting by marinating the chicken and shrimp, then move on to the serving ingredients that need some marinating time (like the Lemony Herbs + Onions on page 154 and Cucumber, Parsley + Red Onion Salad on page 142), and make the halloumi while the shrimp and chicken cook. It's easier than it looks, I promise.

FOR THE KEBABS

3 teaspoons ground cumin

1½ teaspoons ground turmeric

Kosher salt and freshly ground black pepper

1 lemon, zested and halved

3 small garlic cloves, grated or minced

¼ cup thick, full-fat yogurt, such as Greek or Skyr

1½ pounds boneless, skinless chicken thighs, cut into 2-inch cubes

1 pound shrimp, peeled and deveined

¼ teaspoon crushed red pepper flakes

1 teaspoon dried oregano

3 tablespoons olive oil

1 small red onion, thinly sliced

Pan-Seared Halloumi (page 73)

FOR SERVING

Lemony Herbs + Onions (page 154) or **Simple Green Salad** (page 178)

Sliced cucumbers, or **Cucumber, Parsley + Red Onion Salad** (page 142)

Herby Yogurt Dip (page 169)

Toasted pitas or **Za'atar Flatbread** (page 172)

Harissa

Lemon wedges

MAKE THE KEBABS: In a medium bowl, combine 2 teaspoons of the cumin, the turmeric, ½ teaspoon salt, 1 teaspoon black pepper, lemon zest, garlic, and yogurt. Add the chicken and toss to coat. In another medium bowl, combine the shrimp with the remaining 1 teaspoon cumin, the red pepper flakes, oregano, ½ teaspoon salt, and 2 tablespoons of the olive oil.

Heat the broiler to high with a rack 6 inches from the heat source. On a sheet pan, toss the onion with the remaining 1 tablespoon olive oil and season with salt. Keep the onion slightly off-center on the pan. Add the chicken to the right side of the pan, shaking off excess marinade, in a single layer, and cook until the chicken is charred in spots, 6 to 8 minutes. Use tongs to toss the onion and flip the chicken pieces over, and cook for 4 minutes more. Add the shrimp in a single layer to the empty side of the sheet pan and toss the onion again. Rub the cut sides of both lemon halves in the chicken juices, then place them cut-side up in the corner of the pan. Broil until the chicken and shrimp are cooked through, 4 to 5 minutes more. (If any one element is finished early, remove it from the oven while the others continue cooking.) Meanwhile, make the pan-seared halloumi. (Put the pitas on a sheet pan in the oven to toast in the oven's heat when you add the shrimp.)

ARRANGE THE BOARD: Serve the sides and accompaniments directly on a board or in small bowls, as desired. Transfer the chicken, shrimp, and halloumi to a large platter or board (see Tip), along with the red onion and charred lemon halves, and squeeze some of the fresh lemon wedges over everything. Serve immediately.

———

TIP Place toasted pitas on the board first, then spoon the chicken and shrimp on top of the bread, which will soak up the juices better. Or you can place each in small bowls on the board.

NOTE

If you're feeding a strict pescatarian who doesn't want the shrimp and chicken juices potentially mingling, then cook the shrimp in a skillet, about 2 minutes per side.

There's nothing I love more than a good outdoor meal—leisurely snacking and drinking as the sun slowly sets and the weather cools down, like at a picnic or backyard get-together. The recipes in this chapter are easily made at home for any outdoor gathering, whether it's a spread of food laid out on a blanket, on a picnic table, or in your own outdoor space (lucky you!). I've also found that there are two types of picnic planners, ones who enjoy preparing everything ahead of time and ones who would rather let everyone put the meal together themselves by bringing the individual components and a small cutting board and knife. Because of this, you'll find that each recipe comes with two sets of instructions/serving suggestions so that you can arrange the picnic or backyard spread as you wish.

The recipes can also be mixed and matched, especially the salads that get better with time, so don't feel constricted by these suggested pairings.

PICNIC PLANNING

The question to consider before planning a picnic is: will there be forks and plates? Meaning, will everyone use their hands to eat the food or will you move into the realm of salads, where plates and forks will be necessary. If the former, then I'm bringing lots of snacks to round out the sandwiches and finger food: think snap peas, cut watermelon, cherries, blueberries, and so on, that can easily be shared and eaten sans cutlery.

No matter what you choose, remember to have a designated garbage bag and, if you are bringing plates, a kitchen towel, or something you don't mind getting dirty, to wrap up the used plates so they don't get your bag dirty, too. I'm a big fan of deli containers that you can buy in bulk; they are light, easy to store, and inexpensive, and there's no threat of spillage or leaks when transporting.

A quick picnic checklist:

☐ Blanket

☐ Cups

☐ Drinks

☐ Food

☐ Forks/plates (if using)

☐ Napkins

☐ Garbage bag

☐ Music

GRAPEFRUIT
SPARKLER

PALOMA
TWIST

VERMOUTH
SIPPER

AMARO
SPRITZ

DIY DAYTIME DRINKS
The Low-ABV Cocktail Bar

These are my preferred cocktails for daytime sippers—they're light enough that you can enjoy them throughout a long, hot day, and they won't make you crash before sunset. Ranging from bright and refreshing to slightly bitter and warming, these low-ABV cocktails fit any mood. You'll find that they more or less have overlapping ingredients, so you can serve at least two at once by picking one of the more "warming" drinks (like the Amaro Spritz or Vermouth Sipper) and one refreshing counterpart so there's something for everyone. If you want to serve the drinks DIY-style, set up a board with the different garnishes—citrus peels, thinly sliced cucumber, or what have you—with the bottles in cold buckets alongside, label each spirit and write down the recipe measurements on little note cards, and set out a cocktail jigger, ice, and glasses so everyone can make their own. Or you can make large-batch versions of any of these drinks in a carafe and have everyone garnish the drinks themselves.

RECIPE CONTINUES

MY FAVORITE LIQUEURS FOR LOW-ABV COCKTAILS

Sparkling wine: I tended to avoid ordering or making drinks with sparkling wine, as they often taste sweet—until I discovered *crémants*, which I love (and at a price I love). For that reason, I always recommend *crémants* for sparkling wine cocktails (or for drinking by itself, too).

Amaro: Amaro is technically a digestif, meaning it's filled with ingredients that are meant to help you digest a heavy meal. I love amaro after a big dinner (in a mixed drink or simply on the rocks), or if I don't feel like drinking a lot more but want a nightcap. Amaro also works wonderfully when given a spritz-like treatment with sparkling wine, which balances its slight bitterness and depth of flavor.

Grapefruit liqueur: Grapefruit liqueur is undeniably my favorite thing to drink in the summer, and Giffard Pamplemousse is the best out there. It's worth seeking out for these recipes; it's on the sweeter side but more importantly is bright, refreshing, and aromatic.

Vermouth: I first fell in love with sipping sweet vermouth in Barcelona, where it's commonly enjoyed with an orange wedge or with a splash of club soda to lighten it up. Antica Formula is one of the best vermouths, in my opinion, but opt for a local one, if and when you can. The orange wedge (or wheel, if you prefer) helps flavor the drink while also giving you something to snack on at the end.

—— AMARO SPRITZ ——

GLASS: RED WINE OR BALLOON

SERVES 1

2 ounces amaro, such as
Amaro Montenegro

3 ounces sparkling wine,
preferably *crémant*

Orange peel

In an ice-filled glass, combine the amaro
and the wine and serve as such with
a stirrer for a more visually attractive
presentation, or use a bar spoon to quickly
and gently stir together. Twist the peel
over the glass to release the essential oils,
then drop the peel into the drink.

—— GRAPEFRUIT —— SPARKLER

GLASS: COLLINS, HIGHBALL, OR RED WINE

SERVES 1

1 ounce grapefruit liqueur, such as
Giffard Pamplemousse, or
other citrus liqueur

5 ounces sparkling wine,
preferably *crémant*

Cucumber slice or lime peel

In an ice-filled glass, combine the liqueur
and the wine and use a bar spoon to
quickly and gently stir together. Slide the
cucumber slice into the drink. If using
the lime, twist the peel over the glass to
release the essential oils, then drop the
peel into the drink.

PALOMA TWIST
with Cucumber
GLASS: COLLINS

SERVES 1

½ ounce Giffard Pamplemousse
or other grapefruit liqueur

2 ounces tequila

½ ounce grated cucumber
pulp and juice

½ ounce lime juice

Splash of club soda or ginger beer

Lime wheel or peel or thinly
sliced cucumber

In an ice-filled glass, combine the liqueur, tequila, cucumber pulp and juice, and lime juice. Top with a splash of club soda and add the lime wheel.

VERMOUTH SIPPER
GLASS: ROCKS

SERVES 1

2 ounces sweet vermouth,
such as Antica Formula

Splash of club soda (optional)

Orange wedge

In an ice-filled glass, combine the vermouth and the club soda, if using. Garnish with the orange wedge.

THE CRISPY CHICKEN BITES SPREAD
Parmesan & Herb-Baked Chicken + Cabbage Slaw + Yogurt Dip

SERVES 4 TO 6

This spread of chicken strips, slaw, and dip is inspired by a cross between chicken fingers of the '90s and a fried chicken picnic spread. The juicy, flavorful chicken has a cheesy-herb crust with a yogurt marinade that keeps the meat tender. While the suggested dip here is a Dijon-yogurt sauce, you can also choose to serve straight-up mustard (whole grain, Dijon, or honey), or the Herby Yogurt Dip (page 169). And while I love this chicken with a crunchy, slaw-like salad with an acidic dressing, the Garlicky Blistered Green Beans (page 83) would also be a perfect accompaniment.

If you're making this for a picnic or transporting the meal in any way, pack up the chicken, slaw, and dip separately in containers, and then spread them out together on a small board or platter wherever you're serving.

TIP The yogurt helps keep the cutlets moist and tender, and, as they are baked rather than fried, some of the breadcrumbs might not be as crispy as you'd like. If that happens, just broil both sides of the cutlets rather than one. You can also let the chicken marinate in the yogurt mixture covered overnight in the refrigerator before continuing with the rest of the recipe.

FOR THE CHICKEN CUTLETS

¼ cup plus 2 tablespoons thick, full-fat yogurt, such as Greek or Skyr

1 tablespoon Dijon mustard

Kosher salt

1 cup panko breadcrumbs

¼ cup grated Parmesan

1 cup (packed) fresh parsley, dill, or cilantro, finely chopped

1 teaspoon dried oregano

1 teaspoon crushed red pepper flakes

¼ cup olive oil, plus more for the pan

1½ pounds chicken cutlets, or 3 to 4 chicken breasts, halved horizontally

Freshly ground black pepper

FOR SERVING

½ cup thick, full-fat yogurt, such as Greek or Skyr + 1 tablespoon Dijon mustard + salt to taste

Green Cabbage Slaw (recipe follows)

Garlicky White Beans (page 183)

Garlicky Blistered Green Beans (page 83)

Mustard, honey mustard, or ketchup

MAKE THE CHICKEN CUTLETS: Preheat the oven to 425°F. Place one rack in the center and another rack 6 inches from the broiler.

In a medium bowl, combine the yogurt, mustard, and 1 teaspoon salt. In another medium bowl, combine the panko, Parmesan, parsley, oregano, and red pepper flakes. Stir in ¼ cup olive oil until smooth.

Brush a sheet pan with 1 tablespoon olive oil. Pat the chicken dry with a paper towel and lightly season both sides of the cutlets with salt and black pepper. Add the chicken cutlets, one at a time, to the yogurt mixture, tossing to coat well. Shake off any excess yogurt, then dip each cutlet in the breadcrumb mixture to coat it all over. Arrange the chicken on the sheet pan and repeat with the remaining cutlets. (It's okay if they are close together, as they will shrink slightly when cooked.)

Bake on the center rack until the chicken is cooked through and the crust is golden brown, about 15 minutes, depending on the thickness of the cutlets. Flip the cutlets over and transfer the sheet pan to the upper rack. Heat the broiler to high and broil until the crust is even deeper brown (but keep an eye on it so it doesn't burn), 1 to 2 minutes. Let cool slightly before slicing the chicken into bite-size strips. Store in an air-tight container in the refrigerator if not serving immediately. (The chicken will keep for up to 3 days in the fridge.)

MEANWHILE, ARRANGE THE BOARD: In a small bowl, combine the yogurt, mustard, and salt to taste. Arrange the chicken tenders on a board or large platter, and serve the green cabbage slaw and yogurt sauce in bowls to place on the board alongside. Serve any remaining accompaniments directly on the board or in small bowls around the board, as desired.

RECIPE CONTINUES

GREEN CABBAGE SLAW

Inspired by the German *krautsalat*, this slaw has a pleasant acidity from apple cider vinegar and a clean, cool crunch thanks to dill and cucumber. I like my cabbage to stay kind of chunky, but you can also use a mandoline to shred it for a lighter, airier salad. The longer the slaw soaks up the flavors, the better, so you can make it well ahead of time and enjoy it for multiple meals throughout the week or weekend.

1 small head of green cabbage, sliced (about 6 cups)

Kosher salt

½ cup (packed) fresh dill, roughly chopped

2 tablespoons apple cider vinegar

1 tablespoon extra-virgin olive oil

2 Persian cucumbers or other small cucumbers, thinly sliced

Freshly ground black pepper

In a large serving bowl, use your hands to toss the cabbage with 1 teaspoon salt, the dill, vinegar, and olive oil until the cabbage is well dressed. Add the cucumbers and toss to coat. Let sit for 15 minutes before serving, or transfer to an airtight container and refrigerate until ready to serve. Season generously with additional salt and pepper before serving or packing.

THE SANDWICH BOARD

Spicy Turkey Sandwiches & Mozzarella + Avocado Sandwiches

Inspired by my lifelong, unrealized dream of a party sub, these sandwiches can be eaten solo or shared as part of a spread. This way, two sandwiches will be enough for three or four people (especially if you're serving this along with other transportable dishes like the salads on page 142). Or make a large sandwich situation by making both recipes. These two options stick to the gold standards of successful sandwich making: in each case there's a creamy spread, a meat or vegetable filling, a beloved extra condiment, and, of course, some good crusty bread. To serve, you can pack them ahead for travel—see the sidebar below for tips on that—or cut the sandwiches into smaller portions (almost like finger sandwiches, except sub style) and place them on boards with optional dips and extra servings of the ingredients to serve at home.

FOR SERVING

Quick-Pickled Shallots (page 153)

Dijon mustard

Mayonnaise

TIPS FOR PACKING SANDWICHES FOR THE ROAD

If you're bringing these sandwiches anywhere for later (like the beach or a park picnic) and want to make them ahead of time, follow these steps to wrap properly:

Cut the sandwich in half crosswise almost all the way through the bread, leaving it attached. Place the sandwich in the center of a large piece of parchment paper or aluminum foil. Then turn the sandwich so it's laying diagonally on the paper with each end facing a corner, take the opposite corners that the sandwich ends aren't facing, and fold them over the middle of the sandwich. Then fold the remaining corners, like you're wrapping a present, tucking them in to fully wrap the sandwich. Use tape or rubber bands to secure the ends.

SPICY TURKEY SANDWICH

MAKES 2 SANDWICHES

½ recipe **Lemony Herbs + Onions** (page 154), using 1 cup cilantro + adding ½ cup jalapeño, sliced into coins

1 avocado, halved

Juice of 1 lime

Kosher salt

2 (12-inch) Italian sandwich loaves (or any other 12-inch loaves)

1½ teaspoons Dijon mustard

4 ounces provolone or cheddar cheese, sliced

1 pound sliced deli turkey

Make the lemony herbs + onions. In a small bowl, mash the avocado with a fork. Stir in the lime juice and season to taste with salt. Halve both loaves lengthwise directly on the serving board, but keep them intact so they're not fully cut through. Spread the mustard on one side of each loaf and spread the avocado mixture on the other half. Layer the cheese on top of the avocado, fold the turkey slices and layer on top, followed by the lemony herbs + onions. Close each sandwich with the top half of the bread, gently pressing down so that the two pieces adhere, then cut the sandwiches crosswise into smaller pieces or wrap (see sidebar, page 139) if not serving immediately.

VARIATION

Swap the turkey for rotisserie chicken or turn the cucumber + cheddar + parsley combination (page 53) into a sandwich.

MOZZARELLA + AVOCADO SANDWICH

MAKES 2 SANDWICHES

Herby Green Sauce (page 157)

2 (12-inch) Italian loaves (or any other 12-inch loaves)

1 avocado, sliced

1 8-ounce ball fresh mozzarella, torn into bite-size pieces or thinly sliced

1 Persian cucumber or ½ small regular cucumber, thinly sliced or peeled into ribbons

1 cup baby spinach

Make the herby green sauce. Halve both loaves lengthwise, keeping them intact so they're not fully cut through. Layer the avocado on one half of each loaf, followed by the mozzarella. Add the cucumber and spinach, pressing down to ensure everything is compact. Spoon some of the herby green sauce generously over the spinach, close each sandwich with the top half of the bread, and cut the sandwiches crosswise into smaller pieces or wrap (see sidebar, page 139) if not serving immediately.

PICNIC SALAD TRIO

Salads That Get Better with Time

CUCUMBER, PARSLEY + RED ONION SALAD

Crunchy, light, and acidic, this salad is a welcome pairing to serve alongside the Kebab Dinner (page 122) or the Mini Sliders Board (page 102), or on its own as a light summer lunch. The longer you let it sit, the more pickled it becomes as it marinates in the acidic dressing.

SERVES 4

2 tablespoons apple cider vinegar

½ teaspoon Dijon mustard

2 tablespoons extra-virgin olive oil

Kosher salt

¼ teaspoon crushed red pepper flakes

1 small red onion, thinly sliced

1 pound Persian cucumbers or other small cucumbers (5 to 7), thinly sliced

½ cup fresh flat-leaf parsley, roughly chopped or torn

In a large serving bowl or airtight container, combine the vinegar, mustard, and olive oil and whisk until smooth. Season with ½ teaspoon salt, and add the red pepper flakes, onion, cucumbers, and parsley and toss well to coat.

Let sit for at least 15 minutes, or refrigerate for up to 24 hours. Season to taste with salt as needed before serving.

SPICY SMASHED CUCUMBER SALAD

Inspired by the smashed cucumbers found in Chinese cuisine and the Korean marinated cucumber banchan, this version uses Calabrian chili paste, the heat of which yields a similar spice level to this crunchy, cooling snack. Smashing the cucumbers lets the seasoning soak into the craggy bits, but you can also slice them if you prefer a cleaner look. Keep the salad cold until you're ready to eat—it can be made up to a few days ahead of time. It works wonderfully as an appetizer or side dish for a cooling, spicy contrast to dishes like any of the sandwiches on the Sandwich Board (page 139), the Mini Sliders Board (page 102), or the Crispy Snacky Tortilla Board (page 56). The longer you let it sit, the more the cucumber juice will mellow out the heat and thin the dressing, which is nice in a different way.

SERVES 4 TO 6

1 tablespoon Calabrian chili paste

2 tablespoons extra-virgin olive oil

¼ teaspoon sugar

1 garlic clove, grated or minced

1 pound Persian or other small cucumbers (5 to 7), halved lengthwise

Kosher salt

¼ cup fresh mint or basil, roughly torn or chopped (optional)

In a medium serving bowl or airtight container, combine the chili paste with the olive oil, sugar, and garlic and whisk until smooth. Place the cucumbers cut-side down on a sturdy cutting board. Use the flat side of your chef's knife to crush each piece, then cut into bite-size pieces. Add the cucumbers to the dressing and toss to coat. Season to taste with salt and add the herbs, if using. Serve immediately or refrigerate until ready to serve.

AVOCADO + KALE SALAD
with Turmeric Onions

The definition of a salad that gets better with time, this accidentally vegan salad gets a flavor, color, and texture boost from turmeric-y red onions. There's no extra oil added, since the avocado massaged into the kale serves as the dressing, simultaneously tenderizing the tough leaves. If you want to make it non-vegan, it can easily be topped with grated Parmesan or crumbled feta, or even chicken or shrimp.

SERVES 4

½ teaspoon ground turmeric

Kosher salt

Juice of 2 small lemons (about ¼ cup lemon juice)

½ small red onion, thinly sliced

1 bunch curly or lacinato kale, ribs removed and finely chopped

1 teaspoon za'atar

1 avocado, quartered

1 cup croutons, **homemade** (page 95) or store-bought, or 1 cup **Baked Pita Chips** (page 173), broken up (optional)

In a small bowl, combine the turmeric, ¼ teaspoon salt, half of the lemon juice, and the onion. Let sit for at least 15 minutes, tossing occasionally.

In a large bowl, combine the kale with the za'atar, avocado, and remaining lemon juice, squeezing and massaging everything together to tenderize the kale. Season with salt to taste and top with the onion and croutons, if using, immediately, or transfer the salad and the onion to separate airtight containers and refrigerate overnight, then add the onion and croutons just before serving.

HIGHLY TRANSPORTABLE GRAIN BOWL

Farro + Broccoli + Tahini-Parmesan Dressing

SERVES 4

This vegetable-forward grain salad works either hot or cold, making it great for immediate dinners or for preparing ahead and serving for an outdoor get-together. If you're serving the dish hot, then add the cheese on top so it melts slightly, otherwise, add it once the farro is cooled so the cheese doesn't get lost in it. You can also serve it deconstructed by serving the dressed farro with the broccoli, onion, and other toppings on the side.

Kosher salt and freshly ground black pepper

1½ cups semipearled farro

3 tablespoons olive oil, plus more as needed

1 large head broccoli, florets cut into bite-size pieces (about 6 cups)

1 small red onion, cut into ½-inch slices

1 teaspoon ground cumin

½ teaspoon crushed red pepper flakes

Freshly grated zest and juice of 2 lemons

2 tablespoons tahini

2 tablespoons freshly grated Parmesan

¼ cup extra-virgin olive oil

½ cup fresh herbs, such as basil, mint, cilantro, or parsley, roughly chopped or torn

FOR SERVING

Quick-Pickled Jalapeños (page 153)

½ cup crumbled feta

Extra-virgin olive oil

Heat the oven to 400°F and bring a large pot of salted water to a boil.

Add the farro to the pot, reduce the heat to maintain a medium boil, and cook until tender, about 30 minutes. Drain, then return the farro to the pot. Stir in some olive oil to avoid sticking.

Meanwhile, on a sheet pan, coat the broccoli and onion with 3 tablespoons olive oil and season with salt, black pepper, cumin, and red pepper flakes. Roast until the broccoli stems are fork-tender, the florets are crispy, and the onion is soft and silky, 15 to 20 minutes.

Meanwhile, in a small bowl, whisk the lemon zest, lemon juice, tahini, Parmesan, and olive oil until smooth. Stir in half of the herbs and season with salt as needed.

Pour the dressing over the farro and toss to coat. Scrape in the broccoli and onion, tossing to combine. Top with the jalapeños, feta, a drizzle of oil, and the remaining herbs or serve with these items in a small bowl.

GO GREEN PASTA SALAD BOARD

SERVES 4

Not your typical mayo-based pasta salad, this one uses two gems of Italian condiments—pesto and Calabrian chili paste—to flavor the pasta, which is also packed with green vegetables for substance. To serve this on the go, make as written, and then pack extra ingredients from the "for serving" list to offer alongside. If you're serving at home, you can set up the remaining condiments on a board so that everyone can season it as they'd like, adding a bit more pesto or another dollop of chili paste.

FOR THE PASTA

Kosher salt and freshly ground black pepper

1 pound dried mezze rigatoni, penne, orecchiette, or other short pasta

1 bunch asparagus (about 1 pound), trimmed and cut into bite-size pieces

1 bunch broccolini, cut into 1-inch pieces

Olive oil

⅓ cup pesto

Freshly grated zest of 1 lemon, with the lemon halved

1 teaspoon Calabrian chili paste

¼ cup (packed) fresh basil, mint, or parsley, roughly chopped

FOR SERVING

Extra-virgin olive oil

Pesto

Freshly grated Parmesan cheese

Calabrian chili paste

Flaky sea salt

MAKE THE PASTA: Bring a large pot of salted water to a boil. Add the pasta, adjust the heat to maintain a gentle boil, and cook until al dente, about 2 minutes less than the package instructions. About 1 minute before draining the pasta, add the asparagus and broccolini to the pot. Drain everything in a colander, shaking to remove excess water. Then put the cooked pasta and vegetables back in the pot. Return the pot to the stove over low heat. Immediately drizzle in a bit of olive oil. Add the pesto, lemon zest, juice from half the lemon, and chili paste and stir to combine. Top with the herbs, if serving immediately, or remove from the heat and let cool, then transfer to an airtight container.

ARRANGE THE BOARD: Place the extra toppings in small bowls around a board or on a large platter, as desired. Cut the remaining lemon half into wedges. Transfer the pasta to a serving bowl or serve out of the pot on the board.

VARIATION

You can use almost any combination of green vegetables here, in lieu of the asparagus and broccolini (or in addition to), which should all be cut into bite-size pieces. Snap peas, green beans, and/or broccoli all work well.

GO GREEN
PASTA SALAD

HIGHLY
TRANSPORTABLE
GRAIN BOWL

ACCENTS
+ ADD-ONS

Have you ever eaten something and thought, *this is good, but it could use a little something else?* This chapter is all about that something else. Whether it's lemony herbs and onions to add brightness and color or five-minute fruit compotes to top pancakes or toast, these quick recipes will enhance any meal and will hopefully become just as much a part of your go-to recipes as they are a part of mine.

You'll find these "accent recipes," as I like to call them, referred to in many spreads throughout the book, along with variations on how to switch them up to match the recipe at hand or make them your own. And they all take 15 minutes or less.

QUICK-PICKLED SHALLOTS
OR JALAPEÑOS

MAKES ABOUT ½ CUP

The ease of making these quick pickles will hopefully make these a staple for you to always keep in the fridge or whip up whenever you're in the mood. Whether you're using shallots or hot peppers, these pickles are perfect for adding a final touch of acidity and texture to any dish (and a little bit of heat in the case of jalapeños). Set these out for any meals that involve salads, sandwiches, or meats that could use that little extra something else.

½ cup vinegar, such as apple cider, red wine, sherry, or rice wine

¼ teaspoon kosher salt

¼ teaspoon sugar

2 medium shallots, thinly sliced into rings, or 1 or 2 jalapeño, fresno, or Serrano peppers, sliced into rings (see Tip)

In a small bowl, stir together the vinegar, salt, and sugar until the sugar and salt have mostly dissolved. Add the shallots or jalapeños and toss to coat.

Set aside for 15 minutes, stirring occasionally. Serve immediately, or cover and refrigerate for up to 4 days.

TIP If you're sensitive to the heat of chiles, remove the seeds and inner membranes before slicing them.

A NOTE ON QUICK-PICKLING

These pickles—as well as the Lemony Herbs + Onions on page 154—are quick-pickled foods, meaning that the raw ingredients are sitting with an acid of some sort, be it citrus juice or vinegar, for 15 minutes or more, for the purpose of softening the raw flavor from the alliums or chiles and giving it an acidic flavor. Most quick pickles will last up to 4 days covered in the fridge but are not meant for longer storage or use.

If you have store-bought pickled veg on hand, save the pickling liquid even after the pickles are gone. You can add fresh ingredients to the leftover brine, then you don't need to add any vinegar or citrus—just shake well and let sit for at least 15 minutes before using.

LEMONY HERBS + ONIONS

for Topping on Everything

MAKES ABOUT 1 TO 1½ CUPS

This bright herb and onion mixture is a quick way to add a restaurant-quality touch to any dish. The lemon juice cuts the intensity of the raw onions and instead draws out their natural sweetness. Think of it as somewhere in between a garnish and a mini-salad, and it's partly inspired by the combination of lime-pickled onions and cilantro that tops some Mexican dishes. It's also a little ode to my Persian roots, as we almost always had a small plate of fresh herbs, onions, and other ingredients with our meals. It's excellent for piling on top of a key recipe (especially meat, seafood, or roasted veggies) or simply to keep on the side of a board for everyone to use as they please. I like to keep the herbs whole, as I eat them like salad greens, but feel free to chop them—and if you do, make sure to use both the leaves and the tender stems (see page 22), because there's lots of flavor and texture there, too.

TIP This recipe stands up to being made in large batches and stored covered in the fridge for up to 3 days (in fact, the onions will taste even better after a few hours)—just make the onion portion ahead of time and wait until you're ready to serve before adding the herbs, as those are more delicate. You can also refresh leftovers with more herbs.

1 small or ½ large red onion, thinly sliced (about 1 cup)

Juice of 1 lemon (about 3 tablespoons), or more as needed

½ teaspoon kosher salt, plus more as needed

¾ cup fresh parsley and/or cilantro leaves (or ¾ cup chopped)

¼ cup fresh dill, mint, or basil (or ¼ cup chopped)

1 tablespoon extra-virgin olive oil

Freshly ground black pepper

In a small bowl, toss the onion with the lemon juice and ½ teaspoon salt (they won't be submerged and that's okay). Let sit for at least 15 minutes, or cover, transfer to the fridge, and let sit overnight, tossing occasionally.

Just before serving, stir in the herbs and olive oil and toss until the onion and herbs are well coated and glossy with liquid. Taste and season lightly with additional salt, pepper, and lemon juice, as desired.

VARIATION

Add ¼ teaspoon cumin, turmeric, sumac, or crushed red pepper flakes to the mixture after seasoning with salt in the first step.

HERBY GREEN SAUCE

MAKES ABOUT 1 CUP

Like an imaginary love child between Moroccan *chermoula* and Argentinian chimichurri, this green sauce draws on the same bright, zesty flavors of those sauces but adds jalapeño, scallions, and cumin. You can serve this with (or on top of) nearly anything: think meat, seafood, or grilled or roasted vegetables, or spoon it onto a sandwich for an herby, crunchy addition. The sauce is meant to be chunky and unblended, but you can add more olive oil and/or blitz it in a food processor if you want to make it a looser, more drizzly sauce. Feel free to mix it up with the herbs, too, depending on what you have on hand.

¼ teaspoon ground cumin

¼ teaspoon crushed red pepper flakes (optional)

½ teaspoon kosher salt, plus more as needed

½ to 1 jalapeño, seeded and diced, depending on desired heat level

3 scallions, light green and white parts only, chopped

1 cup (packed) mixed fresh soft herbs, such as cilantro, parsley, basil, and/or mint, roughly chopped

Freshly grated zest and juice of 1 large lemon (about 1 tablespoon zest and 3 tablespoons juice)

3 tablespoons extra-virgin olive oil

In a small bowl, add all of the ingredients and stir until combined. Season with additional salt as desired. Serve immediately, or cover and refrigerate for up to 2 days.

SMASHED OLIVES

Meaty Castelvetrano olives often come with a pit, which is easily solved by smashing them with the flat side of a chef's knife (it's actually quite enjoyable to do). While ½ cup of whole olives is often enough for serving as an add-on to a board, you can increase the amount to 1 cup if you're someone who is going to snack on them while you smash them (hi, that's me!). If you prefer other olive varieties to Castelvetrano, go for those instead.

½ to 1 cup Castelvetrano olives

On a cutting board, place the flat side of a chef's knife on an olive, then use the heel of your palm and push down to smash it. The pit will either pop out or you can pull the meat off of the pit. Continue with the remaining olives and transfer them to a small serving bowl.

VARIATION

Spicy Smashed Olives

Prepare the olives as instructed above. In a small serving bowl, add the zest of 1 small lemon, ¼ teaspoon crushed red pepper flakes, paprika, and/or za'atar and drizzle with extra-virgin olive oil. Top with ¼ cup crumbled feta, if desired, and serve.

6 1/2 min

7 min

8 min

JAMMY EGGS
6½-, 7-, or 8-minute eggs

The cook time of a soft-boiled egg is a personal preference, but, depending on other dishes you are eating it with, it can come in handy to know what kind of egg the various cook times will yield: 6½ minutes will get you set egg whites and a runny yolk, while an 8-minute egg will start to approach hard-boiled territory but will maintain a softer, jammier yolk. When you want the yolk to act like a sauce, such as with cooked veggies like mushrooms (page 90) or asparagus (page 92), go for the 6½-minute cook time. But if you want to slice the finished eggs in half and serve them directly on a board for casual snacking, the 7- or 8-minute eggs might be a better option.

4 to 6 large eggs, preferably at room temperature

Flaky sea salt and freshly ground black pepper (optional)

Fill a medium saucepan with enough water to fully submerge the eggs, and bring to a boil.

Using a slotted spoon, carefully lower the eggs into the pot. Adjust the heat to maintain a gentle boil and cook the eggs for 6½ to 8 minutes, depending on your preference, then run them under very cold water for about 30 seconds, or until cool enough to handle. Peel and halve each egg. Sprinkle with salt and pepper, if desired.

QUICK-CHARRED ARTICHOKES

Say hello to your new favorite trick—adding some pantry ingredients to jarred or canned artichokes and charring them in a skillet removes the store-bought taste and infuses them with flavor. Since they are so quick to make, use this as part of any snacking spread, or to top salads or sandwiches.

1 (14-ounce) can artichoke hearts, quartered (see Note)

2 tablespoons olive oil

Kosher salt

¼ teaspoon crushed red pepper flakes

Freshly grated zest of 1 lemon

Freshly ground black pepper

TIP After zesting the lemon, halve it for squeezing over the artichokes, or reserve for another use.

Drain the artichoke hearts, then squeeze out the excess liquid with paper towels. Set the artichokes aside on clean paper towels or a dish towel.

Heat the olive oil in a 12-inch cast-iron or other large, heavyweight skillet over medium-high heat. When the oil is shimmering, add the artichoke hearts and season with salt. Add the red pepper flakes, stirring to coat, and let the artichokes cook, undisturbed, for about 3 minutes, until the bottom is charred in spots. Flip the artichokes and cook about 3 minutes more, until the other side is also charred.

Transfer the artichokes to a small bowl and sprinkle with the lemon zest. Season with additional salt and black pepper to taste, before serving.

NOTE

It's better to buy canned water-packed artichokes for this recipe rather than oil-packed artichokes from a jar. If you use oil-packed, then shake off any excess oil and add the artichokes straight to the pan, without adding more oil.

CARAMELIZED BANANAS

A super quick way to jazz up oatmeal, granola, pancakes, or any breakfast dish, caramelizing bananas gives them a soft, jam-like texture and sweet flavor that will make the start of your day feel a little bit fancy without much effort. Slicing the banana thinly will give it a jammier, more broken-down texture, while thicker slices will retain more of their shape, so choose as you'd like.

2 teaspoons olive oil, ghee, or butter

1 ripe banana, sliced into ¼-inch rounds

In a medium skillet, heat the olive oil or ghee over medium heat until shimmering (or until the butter has melted), swirling the pan to coat. Add the banana and cook, undisturbed, until the edges are golden and easily lift from the pan, 2 to 3 minutes. Use a spatula to flip the banana, turn off the heat, and let the residual heat cook the banana for 1 minute more.

Transfer the banana to a small bowl or plate (or directly on a board) to serve.

ANY-BERRY COMPOTE

SERVES 4

This five-minute compote is a great way to add a touch of juicy sweetness and fruit to whatever you're serving. Simply choose your favorite berry and cook it with a little bit of maple syrup (or agave). It's also a great way to use up any fruit that's more tart than you'd like, but if you have fruit that's especially sweet, feel free to reduce the amount of syrup—just taste as you go. I love to spoon compote over yogurt, ice cream, toast, and pancakes (page 37), or to swirl it into oatmeal (of course it also works great on a cheese board).

6 ounces blueberries, blackberries, or raspberries (about 1 cup), or ½ pound strawberries, hulled and halved, large ones quartered

2 tablespoons maple syrup or agave

In a medium saucepan over medium-high heat, combine the berries and syrup and stir to coat. Cook, stirring occasionally, until the berries have burst and the compote is bubbling, about 5 minutes. (The compote should taste more like the berries than maple syrup.)

Transfer the compote to a four- or six-inch bowl and serve immediately, or transfer to an airtight container and refrigerate for up to 3 days.

VARIATIONS

Add 1 tablespoon freshly grated ginger to the berries and syrup at the start of cooking.

Add 1 tablespoon freshly grated lemon zest after cooking.

Add 1 teaspoon Angostura bitters after cooking.

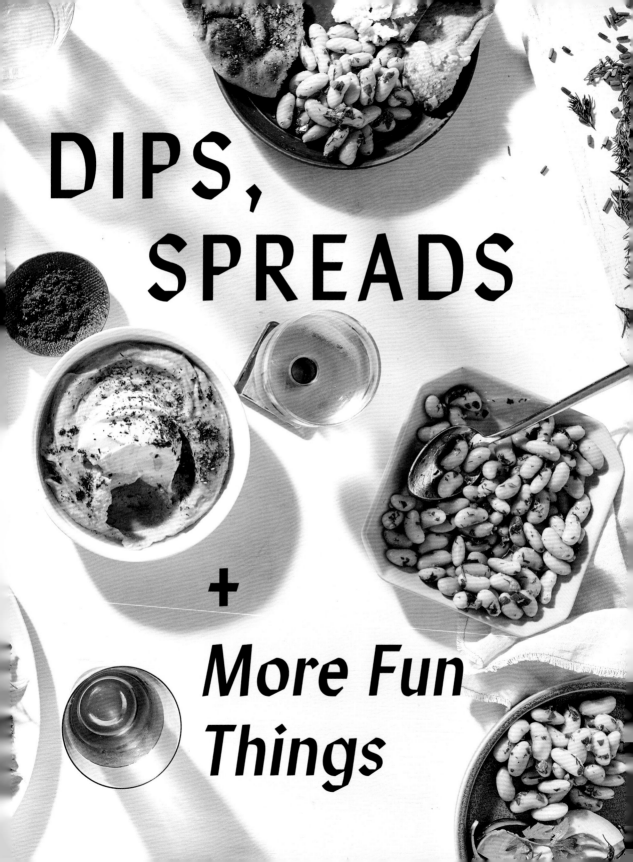

DIPS, SPREADS

+

More Fun Things

Dips, spreads, and simple sides are perfect for putting out for friends with some cocktails or wine to add a cozy, homemade touch. I have a habit of filling up on these snacky things because I love a good dipping situation, but you can try to avoid this by substituting raw, crunchy vegetables—like sliced peppers, snap peas, cucumbers, or carrots—as the "dippers" instead of the suggested breads or pita chips. Aside from dips, you'll also find a few simple salads and vegetable dishes here that are equally quick to throw together. They are wonderful accompaniments to many of the larger spreads in earlier chapters, so you'll also find these recipes referenced throughout the book—they're a great way to round out meals when you're feeding multiple people, and they balance the variety of flavors and textures on any given spread.

HERBY YOGURT DIP

SERVES 2 TO 4

This herb-packed yogurt dip is excellent with the Baked Pita Chips (page 173) or any crackers, but it also works great alongside grilled meat or seafood, or even as a condiment for a burger, sliders (page 102), or a sandwich. You can play with any combo of the herbs (or stick with one), and use the variations below to match this dip to whatever else you're eating. Feel free to get creative with other add-ins, too, to keep this feeling new.

1 cup thick, full-fat yogurt, such as Greek or Skyr

Juice of 1 small lemon or 2 limes (about 2 tablespoons)

½ teaspoon ground cumin

½ cup (packed) fresh mint, dill, cilantro, or parsley, finely chopped

¼ teaspoon kosher salt, plus more as needed

In a small bowl, combine the yogurt, lemon juice, cumin, herbs, and ¼ teaspoon salt. Taste and season with additional salt as desired. Serve immediately, or cover and refrigerate overnight until serving.

VARIATIONS

Harissa Herby Yogurt Dip

Add ¼ to ½ teaspoon harissa to the yogurt mixture and stir until combined (add more harissa depending on your desired heat level).

Cucumber Herby Yogurt Dip

Add 1 diced Persian cucumber or other small cucumber to the yogurt mixture.

RESTAURANT-STYLE HUMMUS

SERVES 2 TO 4

Just like you can brighten up store-bought guacamole with fresh cilantro and a squeeze of lime juice, you can make any store-bought hummus look (and taste) homemade with just a few fresh ingredients, a drizzle of olive oil, and a sprinkle of spices to dress it up. It's best to use a classic flavor of hummus here, one with minimal ingredients—the only things that should really be in the ingredients list are chickpeas, tahini, lemon, salt, and oil (sometimes garlic, too). That way, you'll be more in control of how you season it at home.

1 (10-ounce) container of hummus (preferably a classic/plain variety)

1 tablespoon labneh or other thick, full-fat yogurt, such as Greek or Skyr

⅛ teaspoon za'atar, cayenne, or sumac

1 tablespoon chopped preserved lemon (from about ¼ lemon)

1 teaspoon harissa

Extra-virgin olive oil, for drizzling

FOR SERVING

Za'atar Flatbread (page 172) or **Baked Pita Chips** (page 173)

Sliced cucumbers, radishes, or bell peppers

Divide the hummus between two small bowls. Use a fork to gently whip the hummus, moving in a circular motion to incorporate air into it (this will give it an even smoother and creamier texture, and therefore will look more homemade). Use the bottom of a spoon to smooth the top, then make a well in the center of each serving by pressing the spoon down. In one well, add the labneh and sprinkle with the za'atar. In the other well, add the preserved lemon and harissa. Drizzle with olive oil, then serve.

VARIATIONS

Add any of the following ingredients to one or both wells:
1 tablespoon chopped roasted red peppers
1 tablespoon tahini
1 teaspoon Calabrian chili paste
1 or 2 roasted garlic cloves (plus 1 or 2 additional cloves, chopped, to stir into the hummus before making the well)

ZA'ATAR FLATBREAD

SERVES 2 TO 4

One of my favorite things to do is dress up store-bought flatbread such as naan (or any homemade one, if you're lucky enough to have some) with a little olive oil and za'atar, which makes it the perfect match for any of the spreads or dips in this chapter. I make a habit of keeping store-bought naan in my freezer so I can make this in a pinch.

2 pieces of store-bought naan, or other flatbread

Olive oil

1 teaspoon za'atar

Heat the broiler to high with a rack 6 inches from the heat source.

Arrange the naan on a sheet pan and coat the top and sides of the naan with olive oil. Sprinkle ½ teaspoon za'atar on each piece of naan and use your hands or a brush to coat all over.

Place the sheet pan on the rack under the broiler and cook until the edges of the naan are golden brown, 2 to 3 minutes. Transfer to a board and slice into dippable, bite-size strips or tear into pieces.

BAKED PITA CHIPS
with Sumac

SERVES 2 TO 4

Homemade pita chips are quick and easy and can be jazzed up with various toppings for extra flavor. I love using sumac for pita chips after trying a version at Erewhon Market, a fantastic (and expensive) grocery store in L.A. Sumac, which is the ground powder of sumac berries, has a tart, lemony flavor that complements the chips, but you can also try using spices and blends such as cayenne, cumin, za'atar, or some nice flaky sea salt. If you have leftover chips, break them up to use in the Cucumber, Parsley + Red Onion Salad (page 142) as a play on *fattoush,* or add them to the Avocado + Kale Salad with Turmeric Onions (page 144). You can also reheat the chips for a few minutes before using to crisp them up again.

3 small pita bread rounds (white or whole-wheat)

3 tablespoons olive oil

1 teaspoon kosher salt

2 teaspoons sumac

Flaky sea salt (optional)

Preheat the oven to 350°F and have two sheet pans ready.

Cut the pita rounds into quarters using scissors or a knife, then cut each quarter in half to form 8 wedges. Open each wedge to separate it into 2 thin pieces.

Divide the olive oil and the pita slices between the sheet pans, and toss the pita to lightly coat with the oil. (If you are using just one sheet pan, do this in batches.) Arrange the pita slices in a single layer on each sheet pan.

In a small bowl, combine the kosher salt and sumac. Sprinkle the sumac mixture over the pita wedges and use your hands to rub it in, ensuring the wedges are evenly coated. Transfer the sheet pans to the oven and bake until the pita chips are crispy and golden brown all over, about 15 minutes, rotating the baking sheets and flipping the chips over halfway. Let cool slightly before using (they will continue to crisp a bit as they cool) and sprinkle with flaky salt, if desired.

TWO-MINUTE FETA DIP

SERVES 2 TO 4

I first started making this dip in my early twenties, mostly because I always had feta in the fridge and needed to throw something together when friends came over, and I hadn't planned that well in advance. A drizzle of olive oil, some red pepper flakes, and a sprinkle of lemon zest work like magic to turn feta into a salty, slightly spicy dip that everyone will polish off very quickly. (Fortunately it takes about two minutes to put together, which means it's also easy to replenish on the spot.) Since the dip is fairly simple, the key to its success is the quality of the feta. My personal preference is Bulgarian feta packed in the brine because it's creamier and tangier than its counterparts, but any feta in the brine is preferable to feta in a dry package or pre-crumbled feta.

1 cup loosely crumbled feta

Extra-virgin olive oil

¼ teaspoon crushed red pepper flakes

Finely grated zest of ½ lemon

FOR SERVING

Baked Pita Chips (page 173)

Crusty bread, warm pita, or **Za'atar Flatbread** (page 172)

In a small serving bowl, add the feta and drizzle with enough olive oil to create a shallow pool at the bottom of the bowl. (The oil should not completely cover the feta, but it should still be enough to make it feel more like a marinated feta dip than just drizzled feta.) Sprinkle with the red pepper flakes and lemon zest, and serve with pita chips and/or bread.

SCALLION LABNEH

SERVES 2 TO 4

Labneh is an ingredient that I love so much it's hard for me to have it in the fridge, as I am constantly tempted to eat spoonfuls of it every time I open the door. As a kid, I would make hot pita and labneh sandwiches as an after-school snack, loving the way the rich strained yogurt became melty and creamy between the toasted pita. Now as an adult, I eat it in tomato-labneh toasts (page 52) and in this form it is like a creamier, richer version of scallion cream cheese (but with a smoother texture). Use it whenever you want a thicker version of the Herby Yogurt Dip (page 169), with a little more punch. And if you ever want a labneh dip without scallions, sprinkle the labneh with a drizzle of olive oil and a little za'atar, sumac, ras el hanout, or your favorite spice blend.

2 scallions, light green and white parts only, thinly sliced

1 cup labneh

Extra-virgin olive oil, for drizzling

In a small bowl, stir the scallions into the labneh until combined. Drizzle with olive oil and serve.

TWO SUPER SIMPLE SALADS

That You Can Serve with Almost Anything

SERVES 2 TO 4

SIMPLE GREEN SALAD

One of the many traditions I love about restaurants in Europe is the simple green salad. In France, it's usually dressed with a bistro vinaigrette, similar to this one; or sometimes in Italy, the greens will arrive at your table with bottles of olive oil and vinegar for you to dress it yourself. It's a great way to add some green to a meal without a lot of work. But if you like a more textured salad, you can expand on this by adding simple things like Parmesan, feta, tomatoes, cucumbers, fresh herbs, or whatever you have on hand—I recommend keeping it minimal though, for a bright, fresh presentation and a goes-with-anything appeal.

SERVES 2 TO 4

½ teaspoon Dijon mustard

1 tablespoon vinegar (such as sherry or balsamic) or lemon juice

2 tablespoons extra-virgin olive oil

1 small head tender lettuce, such as red leaf, butter, or baby gem

Flaky sea salt and freshly ground black pepper

In a medium bowl, whisk the mustard and vinegar until combined. Gradually whisk in the olive oil until smooth. Toss with the lettuce. Season to taste with salt and pepper and serve immediately.

——— ARUGULA SALAD ———

Simple and flavorful as this salad is, you could also add some Quick-Pickled Shallots (page 153), halved cherry tomatoes, sliced cucumbers, or Marinated Chickpeas (182).

SERVES 2 TO 4

1 tablespoon vinegar (such as apple cider, red wine, or sherry) or lemon juice

2 tablespoons extra-virgin olive oil

4 cups baby arugula

¼ cup grated or crumbled Parmesan

Flaky sea salt and freshly ground black pepper

In a medium bowl, whisk the vinegar and olive oil until smooth. Add the arugula and toss to combine, then add the cheese. Season to taste with salt and pepper and serve immediately.

NOTE

With both of these salads, you can assemble the dressings in the bowl you intend to serve the salad in so that you can save on the number of dishes to wash. Because both of these use tender, more delicate leaves, you want to dress them right before serving.

AVOCADO SALAD

SERVES 2 TO 4

Inspired by the Cuban salad of red onion and slices of avocado, this version is dressed up with herbs and can be eaten on its own—or with some crusty bread, like a DIY avocado toast of sorts, the Za'atar Flatbread on page 172, or served alongside meat or seafood or as part of a larger spread. To bulk it up, serve it on a bed of lightly dressed arugula, baby gem lettuce, or pea shoots (all drizzled with a little olive oil will be perfect). Make sure the avocados are not overly ripe and mushy; you want ones that are firm and *just* yield to the touch, as opposed to ones that sink to the touch or are rock hard.

Lemony Herbs + Onions
(page 154)

¼ teaspoon ground cumin

¼ teaspoon crushed red pepper flakes

3 firm avocados, thinly sliced

Flaky sea salt and freshly ground black pepper

In a small bowl, toss the lemony herbs + onions with the cumin and red pepper flakes. Set aside.

Place the avocado slices on a large plate or shallow bowl. Top with most of the lemony herbs + onions mixture and season with salt and black pepper. (Taste the salad for acidity, too—if it needs more, then you can pour some of the leftover liquid from the lemony herbs over it.) Serve the remaining lemony herbs + onions on the side.

MARINATED CHICKPEAS

SERVES 2 TO 4

When dressed with a quick marinade of vinegar, miso, and herbs, chickpeas add a pop of flavor and substance to any meal. The miso provides a wonderful depth and umami flavor to the chickpeas that make them surprisingly flavorful. While the chickpeas need 15 minutes or so to marinate and develop enough flavor, they only get better with time. I like to make a full batch, eat some right away, then store the rest in the fridge for other uses later in the week—the chickpeas are phenomenal on salads, or you can turn them into a bulked-up side dish with quinoa and fresh herbs.

3 tablespoons sherry vinegar or apple cider vinegar

½ teaspoon white miso

½ teaspoon Dijon mustard

¼ teaspoon crushed red pepper flakes

3 tablespoons extra-virgin olive oil

¼ cup (packed) fresh parsley or cilantro, roughly chopped

2 (15-ounce) cans chickpeas, drained and rinsed

Kosher salt and freshly ground black pepper

In a large bowl, whisk the vinegar, miso, mustard, red pepper flakes, and olive oil until smooth. Add the herbs and chickpeas and toss to coat. Season to taste with salt and black pepper, then set aside for at least 15 minutes or refrigerate if not using immediately.

VARIATIONS

Add any or all of the following when tossing the chickpeas in the marinade:
1 grated garlic clove
¼ teaspoon cumin, sumac, or za'atar
Zest of 1 small lemon or lime
1 or 2 scallions, light green and white parts, thinly sliced

GARLICKY WHITE BEANS

SERVES 2 TO 4

Think of these as half–bean dip, half–bean salad—they work equally well scooped up with bread or pita chips or added on top of other things (like toast or salad greens like arugula). Depending on the kind of spread you're serving this with, try topping the beans with cheese, such as crumbled feta, torn mozzarella, or ricotta salata.

Herby Green Sauce (page 157)

1 tablespoon olive oil, plus more for drizzling

2 garlic cloves, grated or minced

2 (15-ounce) cans white beans, such as cannellini or great northern, drained and rinsed

¼ teaspoon kosher salt, plus more as needed

1 lemon, cut into wedges (optional)

Make the herby green sauce and set aside.

Heat the olive oil and garlic in a large skillet over medium heat until the garlic is fragrant and starts to sizzle, about 45 seconds. Add the white beans and ¼ teaspoon salt, stirring to coat with the oil, until the beans are warmed through, about 2 minutes. (If the beans seem dry, add another tablespoon or so of olive oil.)

Transfer the bean mixture to a serving bowl and pour the herby green sauce over them, stirring to coat the beans. (It's okay if some of the beans get mashed.) Season with additional salt as desired, and squeeze a bit of lemon juice over the beans, if using. Drizzle with additional olive oil before serving.

VARIATIONS

Spicy White Beans

Omit the herby green sauce. Before adding the beans to the skillet, add ½ to 1 teaspoon harissa or Calabrian chili paste to the garlic.

Garlicky White Bean Salad

Add 1 cup baby arugula to the beans when warm to lightly wilt. Drizzle with extra-virgin olive oil and toss.

ACKNOWLEDGMENTS

Thank you!

Thank you to all of Clarkson Potter for making this beautiful book possible. It's been a wonderful experience working with such smart, talented, and detail-oriented people. Lydia O'Brien, thank you for being such a great editor on this project. I loved our "live" chats, voice messages, and how much we both love leaving notes. Thank you to Stephanie Huntwork and Mia Johnson, too. And a big thanks to everyone involved in the publication of this book and getting it out into the world, including Natalie Yera, Chloe Aryeh, Abby Oladipo, Kim Tyner, Natalie Blachere, and the PRH Sales team. And thank you to Adriana Stimola.

To the fabulous photoshoot team—I love you and you're stuck with me forever. Julia Gartland, your photos, lighting, and overall wonderful self made this book shine. Barrett Washburne, you talented, talented man! So grateful for your styling skills on set and to have you in my life. Brooke Deonarine, love your color pairings, props, and picnic dresses. Thank you to Spencer Richards, Daniel Restrepo, and Don Purple for being all-around talented, fun, and kind people. You all made this book come to life!

A cookbook is only as good as the recipes, and I owe a huge thank-you to everyone who helped test these out. Lisa Nicklin, you are an all-star. Every recipe is the best version of itself thanks to you. To my family and friends, to say that I was overwhelmed by the offers (and excitement!) to test recipes is underselling how I felt—you guys are seriously the best. I cannot express how much fun it was to receive your detailed notes and feedback—I'm so grateful for your support and how much you love food! Thank you to team Katie Carey + Ann Bermont, team Nichole Ferrara + Ben Bernstein, Joni Colburn, Diana Perez, Aaron Krieger, Nicole Jackson, Molly Ahuja, Maryse Chevriere, Amanda Bassen, Rebecca Clareman, Hannah Howard, Barbara Buck-Aronica, and Lauren Shockey—this is in no particular order, as you are all amazing.

For everyone who helped make this book the beauty that it is in their own way: Robby, it was amazing to have your gorgeous ceramics from Robert Siegel Studio to shoot the food on. So many of the colorful and thoughtful linens are from the fabulous Atelier Saucier, so thank you Nikki and Stacey for sending us some to use. And thank you to Kaj Hakkinen, cofounder of Back Bar Project, for introducing me to Giffard Pamplemousse, which I now am obsessed with drinking.

I also don't know where I would be without the supportive, kind, and wonderful friends and family in my life. A huge thank-you to Diana Perez, Ali Rosen, Molly Ahuja, Laura Sweeting, and Ben Israel for inspiring me to make spreads in the first place. Love you all. And also thank you to Michael Manotas-McCafferty for always having a boozy suggestion when I need it.

Ashley Fahr, my lovely sister, thank you for patiently listening to me think out loud about recipe combinations, troubleshooting with me when it didn't work out as planned, and generally listening to me whine when I needed to—and then suggesting that I hire someone to do that (lol). A big thanks as always to my parents for cheering me on and instilling in me a deep love for food and sharing it with others.

I am a lucky lady, so thank you all for that—and for buying this book.

INDEX

Published in the United States by Clarkson Potter/Publishers,
an imprint of Random House, a division of Penguin Random
House LLC, New York.
ClarksonPotter.com
RandomHouseBooks.com

CLARKSON POTTER is a trademark and POTTER with colophon is a
registered trademark of Penguin Random House LLC.

Library of Congress Cataloging-in-Publication Data is available
upon request.

ISBN 978-0-593-23624-6
Ebook ISBN 978-0-593-23625-3

Printed in China

Photographer: Julia Gartland
Photography Assistant: Daniel Restrepo
Food Stylist: Barrett Washburne
Food Stylist Assistant: Spencer Richards
Prop Stylist: Brooke Deonarine
Prop Stylist Assistant: Don Purple

Editor: Lydia O'Brien
Designer: Mia Johnson
Production Editor: Abby Oladipo
Production Manager: Kim Tyner
Compositor: Merri Ann Morrell
Copy Editor: Natalie Blachere
Indexer: Elizabeth Parson
Marketer: Chloe Aryeh
Publicist: Natalie Yera

10 9 8 7 6 5 4 3 2 1

First Edition